C000173103

EARNING YOUR LIVING WITH ANIMALS

BY THE SAME AUTHOR

Okavango Adventure

EARNING YOUR LIVING WITH ANIMALS

Jeremy Mallinson

Foreword by Gerald Durrell

DAVID & CHARLES
NEWTON ABBOT LONDON NORTH POMFRET (VT)
VANCOUVER

ISBN 0 7153 6760 9

Set in 11 on 13pt Garamond and printed in
Great Britain by Latimer Trend & Company Ltd Plymouth
for David & Charles (Holdings) Limited
South Devon House Newton Abbot Devon

Published in the United States of America
by David & Charles Inc
North Pomfret Vermont 05053 USA

Published in Canada
by Douglas David & Charles Limited
3645 McKechnie Drive West Vancouver BC

In fondest love
of
Julian and Sophie Jayne
in the hope that the
animal kingdom
will mean as much to them

Contents

Foreword

I am delighted that a book like this has been written at last. Years ago, when I first started to go on animal collecting expeditions and was unwise enough to write about my experiences, my mailbag suddenly increased enormously. On an average I would get some five or six letters a day asking for my advice on how to be an animal collector. Later, when I appeared for a brief period on television, my mail increased to twenty letters a day asking my advice on how to work with animals. Later still, when my faithful readers learned that I had established my own zoological gardens, my mail increased to a steady fifty a day, from people asking how to become animal collectors, game wardens or members of the staff of my zoo. Every sub-adult male and female in the United Kingdom and the Commonwealth, it seemed, wanted to work with animals. This flood of mail continues to this day, but now, with the publication of this book, I can face it with some sort of equanimity, for instead of having to write long and detailed letters to people, I shall simply advise them to consult this invaluable reference work.

I have known Jeremy Mallinson for a number of years and I know the meticulous devotion and the hard work that he gives to his job with a large and varied collection of wildlife. He has used the same meticulous approach in his preparation of this book. In much of it he speaks from personal experience and, when this was lacking, he got the help and advice of experts in that particular field. The result is a concise and invaluable book, the only one of its kind I am aware of that deals with such a wide variety of careers with animals, embracing, as it does, everything from cats to cattle, from dolphins to bushbabies. This is a book that should be in every school library, for the youngsters of school-leaving age will find it invaluable in choosing a career with animals.

So many young people, dazzled by the attractions of working with animals, tend to think only of the highlights and to overlook the other side of things. They forget that, as well as being a great privilege and pleasure, it can also be frustrating, boring, dirty and damned hard work as well. This, Jeremy Mallinson has made patently clear. He has described every aspect and given a very fair picture of the advantages and disadvantages of the various careers which will be of enormous help to any young person.

GERALD DURRELL

Introduction

A child's passion for animals is mirrored in his eyes as he gazes for the first time at puppies and kittens in a pet-shop window or when, on a farm, he sees new-born calves, lambs, piglets or perhaps a foal. The yearning to touch or hold a young animal appears to be instinctive during a child's formative years. His efforts to persuade his parents to let him have a pet of his own will probably be more successful if he starts off with a white rat, golden hamster or guinea-pig. Then, providing his initial enthusiasm does not wane, he will find it easier to introduce other animals into the home.

From this stage, the extent to which he is going to involve himself with animals follows the natural course of elimination and selection. Taking the dog for a walk, feeding the cat, gathering grass for the rabbit, or looking after a pony, are all part of the young animal-lover's growing-up cycle.

Before enlarging on the many potential careers with animals which are open to young people leaving school, let me say something about my own somewhat unorthodox approach to working in this field.

I had experienced owning white mice, a rabbit, a black kitten, taking other people's dogs for a walk, riding at my preparatory school, and breeding Samoyeds in my teens. On leaving school I set out on a military career in Central Africa with the aim of seeing as much wildlife as possible at the same time. During this period I travelled widely—in Rhodesia, Zambia, Malawi, Zaire, Botswana and South Africa. I came to love the African continent and started to worry about the dangers which threatened its countless fascinating species of animals as 'civilisation' intruded upon their ancient territories.

On my return home, there were a number of careers open to me, but as I weighed up the pros and cons of what I really wanted to do, I came to the conclusion that my greatest satisfaction in life was during my time spent with animals. I realised that somehow, on whatever terms, I needed to be working with them. They could be wild or domesticated, but in one way or another animals had to be at the centre of my life.

First-hand experience of livestock farming in Dorset and a kennel management course in Surrey helped to pave the way for my fifteen years of involvement and dedication to the work being done at Gerald Durrell's Jersey Wildlife Preservation Trust.

In the following pages, I have outlined the different types of jobs open to someone who is really keen to make a career out of working with animals, and in some instances specialists have given a personal account of the nature of their work. In this way, it is hoped that the reader will gain a real feeling of involvement in the career concerned, and acquire an understanding which will act as a guide, as well as helping to prevent any subsequent disillusionment. It appears that people often embark on a career with animals without being fully aware of the varied aspects and ramifications of the work in front of them. It must be taken into consideration, when choosing such a career, that a job may involve a twenty-four-hour day and a seven-day week. It is important for the candidate to have a healthy respect for all animals, and at the same time not to become over-sentimental about them. A spirit of enthusiasm and a deep concern for their welfare are essential qualities. In my own view, the cultivation of understanding and mutual respect between man and beast creates a relationship which, once achieved, is impossible to surpass.

CHAPTER ONE
Dogs

BOARDING KENNELS

A career as a kennelman or kennelmaid at a boarding establishment may have its limitations, but the daily work can be full of interest and enjoyment, providing he or she has the welfare of the boarders at heart. School leavers as well as recruiting students are taken on by most boarding kennels during the holiday periods at Easter, summer and Christmas when people going away want to leave their dogs in a sympathetic home from home.

I remember how much I enjoyed a three-month kennel management course in Surrey. On my arrival, I was greeted by 150 vociferous boarders and by the end of the first week had acquired many friends. I learnt how to sum up a dog on introduction, how temperaments clashed, and how to disarm bullying breeds without loss of face to either. An excellent training, I thought, for any young embassy official.

There were characters like Scamp, a mongrel sheepdog from the Battersea Dogs Home. His winning ways had won the hearts of two wealthy people who had sent him on holiday to the kennels. He wagged his tail when angry and growled when pleased—a truly mixed-up canine. A borzoi belonging to the kennels would race across the exercising paddock as effortlessly as an Arab filly, frequently pursued by a prick-eared and breathless Yorkshire terrier.

A basset hound, with long drooping ears and bloodshot eyes, would shamble off pessimistically on a seemingly fruitless course, eventually stumbling to a standstill and drooling in ecstasy at finding a treasure-chest of smells the others had overlooked. A miniature English bulldog, who had a passion for gulping up the muddiest of puddles, was one of the many dogs with whom I fell in love. When it was time for a boarder to return to its owner, I was frequently heartbroken, for at this stage of my career I had not mastered the art of avoiding over-sentimental attachment to the animals under my charge.

A typical day's work

08.00 Work begins. A preliminary check round the boarders to see that all is well. This is followed, wherever possible, by allowing them into outside runs.

08.30 Cleaning the indoor kennels commences, taking approximately six units at a time. If the weather is suitable, the dogs are confined to the outside runs. Beds or baskets and blankets are removed to be aired and shaken. The kennels are swept, then mopped over with a non-toxic detergent. Water dishes are scrubbed out and refilled. Food dishes are removed for cleaning. By the time the sixth kennel is cleaned, the floor of the first is dry, so the bed and bedding can be replaced and the dog allowed inside again.

10.15 By this time, each inside kennel has been thoroughly cleaned, and the dog is able to run freely between inside and outside accommodation. In damp or very cold weather, the boarders are confined indoors.

10.30 The dogs are brushed and combed. During this time a kennelman or kennelmaid really gets to know each dog as an individual. I have always sensed a feeling of elation when a dog has greeted me in a friendly way, even when it has not enjoyed being groomed.

At the kennels where I studied, a boarder was always given a bath the day before leaving for home. This necessitated applying a shampoo diluted with warm water, and several rinses. After the dog was rubbed down with a coarse towel an electric hair-dryer was switched on. The dog's reaction to this machine often created a near riot, but the majority succumbed and became bewitched by the currents of warm air through their coats.

12.00 The food dishes collected earlier are cleaned, and the daily rations prepared in each dog's individual dish. If frozen meat is to be the meat ration of the day, a sufficient amount will have been taken out of the deep freeze the previous evening and placed in a quantity of gravy to soak. The meat and gravy are mixed with dog biscuits at a ratio of 60 per cent meat and 40 per cent biscuits. The quantity of meat is related to the size of the dog, as well as sometimes to its fussiness. Generally speaking, any boarder arriving with an accompanying brief to say it would only eat a certain type of meat would often accept any brand, once it realised that fastidiousness would not lead to endearment. There were, of course, some who insisted on a particular type of meat, with a degree of dedication that a man might have for a brand of malt whisky.

12.40 The main meal of the day is taken round, much to the welcoming delight of all the boarders.

14.00 The early part of the afternoon is taken up by exercising the boarders outside their individual kennels. Compatible dogs may be put in a large fenced-in paddock, so that they can tear about and work off any surplus energy. Others less sociable may be taken for a circuit walk on leads. After the exercising period, the kennel runs are cleaned out and faeces removed from the paddocks.

16.45 All the dogs are returned to their respective kennels and by 17.30 are secure for the night. Most of them are given biscuits and the odd tit-bit, such as chocolate drops, followed by a final good-night pat. Water dishes are checked to ensure they are full of clean water for the night.

19.30 A final check of all the boarders is made before the lights in the kennels are switched off.

Numerous other jobs have to be worked in with the daily routine, such as the thorough cleaning of a kennel after a boarder has left for home, so that it is ready to welcome another guest. Some time has also to be spent with the dog owners, who are anxious to tell you all about their pets' likes and dislikes and, when coming to collect them, want to know what their dogs have been up to while in the kennels.

Boarders are not usually accepted unless an owner signs a certificate of agreement before leaving a dog on the premises. Dogs are boarded at owner's risk, and have to be in good health before being accepted. A copy of the certificate of inoculation of immunisation against distemper and hardpad must be produced. In order not to unsettle them, dogs are not usually allowed off the premises during the boarding period, but can often be visited by their owners at the discretion of the kennel manager.

The weekly visit of the veterinary surgeon may reveal some problems requiring daily treatment. Drugs prescribed for eyes, nose, mouth, throat, ears, skin, worms, diarrhoea and constipation are administered by the kennel staff.

Kennelmaid training

The one-year course at the Bellmead Kennelmaid Training School at Old Windsor in Berkshire gives thorough practical and theoretical instruction in all branches of kennel work. In addition to general care and management of the dog, the course includes tuition in anatomy, nutrition, whelping, nursing and first aid, breeding and showing, stripping and clipping. Lectures are given by a veterinary surgeon, and practical experience is gained in the kennels under the supervision of qualified staff. Demonstrations and outings are arranged for additional interest and instruction.

Examinations are held termly and at the end of the year. A certificate is awarded on graduation. Students are accepted from school-leaving to twenty-five years of age. They should have a reasonable standard of education, but 'O' level passes are not required. A syllabus will be sent by the principal of the training school on request.

A student graduating from a kennelmaid training course of this nature has a very interesting career in front of her, including senior positions in large boarding kennels, assisting veterinary surgeons in quarantine kennels, and the breeding and showing of pedigree dogs. With this type of background, anyone with an ambition to establish a boarding kennel should, by dedicated work, be able to make a success of such a venture, for there will always be a real need for dog hotels run by a professional and sympathetic team.

QUARANTINE KENNELS

A high percentage of quarantine kennels are run by veterinary surgeons. This is probably due to the fact that a quarantine station must by law be visited daily by a veterinary surgeon to ensure that a disease, such as rabies, can be detected as soon as the first signs are apparent.

A kennelmaid working at such an establishment has the opportunity and benefit of learning a great deal about the diagnosis of disease, parasites, and methods of treatment, as well as experiencing some aspects of animal nursing.

The cleaning, feeding and watering routine is similar to that of a boarding kennel. The exercise potential for the dogs is often limited, however, due to the necessity of minimising the risk of cross-infection to animals not under quarantine restrictions.

BREEDING AND SHOWING

There are over 100 breeds of pedigree dog recognised by the Kennel Club. Most of these have individual clubs, which are enthusiastically supported by their members.

Dog breeding is mostly done by small kennels, some of which also board dogs to provide their 'bread and butter'. Other people may have only two or three dogs, breeding them as a part-time paying hobby. Very few people breed dogs on a large enough scale for it to be financially viable. Establishments like the Bowesmoor Kennels in Bexley, Kent, offer a comprehensive service for dogs—breeding, boarding, trimming and training—the latter also including the handlers. Many dogs trained by the Bowesmoor Kennels have been exported to Africa and other continents whilst others have been sent all over Britain to police forces, prison services, security firms, and local councils. These kennels supply anything from a qualified guard dog to a cuddly pup and, at the height of the breeding season, there may be as many as eighty dogs on the premises.

The breeding of dogs on a commercial basis for research purposes quite rightly causes a great deal of concern among dog lovers. The removal of certain parts of the anatomy so as to mute the dog's protestations in the laboratory emphasises the tragedy of a situation where the dog family is used solely as merchandise, no thought being given to the puppies' future welfare.

Participation in championship shows is almost essential for any registered kennel that is ambitious to succeed with a particular breed. Long-term breeders realise that, if they are to maintain some champions or championship-certificate winners on the three-generation pedigree sheet which accompanies each puppy sale, time must be spent competing at shows up and down the country. A splash of pedigree names, inked out in red on the pedigree sheet, enables the breeder to charge more for the dog sale or stud fee. It also confirms that the breeder is producing stock at a high level by adhering to the rigid scale of points set down for a particular breed. The preparation of dogs for the show is as important as the day itself. Grooming, handling, training the dog to walk and stand properly in the show ring—also stripping and clipping when necessary—all require a lot of practice and professionalism.

GUIDE DOGS FOR THE BLIND

The Guide Dogs for the Blind Association employs staff in three categories: as kennelmaids, whose duties are to care for the dogs generally; training assistants, whose work involves the elementary training of dogs; and fully qualified mobility instructors who undertake the advanced training of dogs and teach blind people how to use them.

Vacancies in each of these groups are limited because of the size of the organisation. Recruitment is normally by advertisement although the association does receive a large number of requests from girls wishing to be kennelmaids.

Guide-dog mobility instructors

The post of mobility instructor is restricted to single men between the ages of eighteen and twenty-five. They must be prepared to undertake a three-year apprenticeship course at one of the association's training centres. The syllabus includes kennel management, dog selection and training, elementary veterinary practice, assessment of dog requirement for blind people and the instruction of blind people in handling guide dogs.

Salaries are allied to the Burnham scale for teachers, plus certain allowances for the teaching of blind people. Applicants should have at least three 'O' levels, including English, and must be of average height and good physical health—extensive walking is involved which may range from ten to twenty miles a day. They need to be of strong sensitivity and imagination in order to understand the difficulties of blind people and to possess the patience necessary for the training of dogs.

A personal account of some twelve years spent working for the association, and nine years as a guide-dog mobility instructor, is provided by Mr Nigel Albright. During that time he has instructed between 100 and 120 guide-dog owners and been involved with almost 250 dogs:

'Of the three-year apprenticeship the first few months are spent in the kennels where the apprentice learns how to care for dogs and how to identify and treat their basic ailments. The kennels have a capacity of 120 dogs.

'All apprentices are required to live in at the Training Centre for the major part of their apprenticeship. Whilst working in the kennels they are required to work the same hours as kennelmaids. This means starting at 7 o'clock in the morning.

'After their time in the kennels apprentices become a part of the Early Training Unit under the direct supervision of the ETU supervisor. From now on they follow the same working hours as the training staff. In the ETU they learn not only how to handle dogs and what form the training takes, but also how to assess the temperament of the dogs—which are good points and which are not.

'Apprentices are also seconded to classes for limited periods so that they may observe how the students are instructed, what sort of common problems occur and how they are dealt with.

'At the end of six months, apprentices have a fairly broad idea of the work involved and how to deal with blind people. At this time and whilst they are still in the ETU they take a written examination. Presuming that this is passed they then officially become trainers and soon afterwards will leave the ETU and be put under the supervision of an instructor whom they will likely work with until they qualify. Whilst under the instructor, the trainer will learn the most important aspects of the work. Under close supervision he will train his own dogs and then train them with students. His first class will probably consist of two students.

'As he nears the end of his three-year apprenticeship the trainer will take a qualification exam, which in combination with the number of students trained will decide whether he will become an instructor.

'All dogs eligible for training must first go through the ETU. They are generally around ten months old and during their two-month stay are assessed to determine whether they are temperamentally suitable for the work. Those which are accepted for training undergo pre-training before being handed over to instructors and trainers for three months' advanced training.

'The ETU is also responsible for the puppy-walking scheme in our area. The scheme involves putting young puppies with suitable members of the public until they are old enough to come to the training centre at around ten months old.

'The unit is staffed by a number of training assistants, mostly girls, some of whom were previously kennelmaids at Cleve. As already mentioned, apprentice trainers also spend a period of time on the ETU. The unit is supervised by a senior instructor.

'The dogs, having passed through the ETU are taken by instructors and trainers for their three months' advanced work—at the end of which they will be trained with blind people (students).

'There are eleven instructors and trainers at Cleve, working in four groups. Each group is composed of an instructor and one or more trainers. The maximum number in any group is three, each person having between six and eight dogs each.

'A class is composed of eight or twelve students who are residential during their one-month training with us. During that time they must learn not only how to handle the dogs, but also how to care for and feed them. At the end of the class the students pay a nominal fee of 50p for their dogs. Each dog is worth £500 by the time it has finished training.

'We now have in the region of 2,000 guide-dog owners working in Great Britain and the Republic of Ireland. We try to see each of these at least once a year working in their own home area. On these visits we observe a sample of the work and offer advice where we think it is either helpful or necessary.

'Each training centre has an allotted area to cover and within these areas the centres are also responsible for interviewing people who have applied for a guide dog.'

A working day

'A typical working day will start when I meet my associate instructor, Paul Master, at the kennels. We roughly plan the day ahead. This is mainly based on the amount of experience the dogs have had so far, combined with the number of items which remain to be covered in the time left available before the class.

'The dogs we wish to take on the first "trip" are selected and supervised into one of the large, specially adapted vans. Since we do not have suitable training conditions on our doorstep we are obliged to transport the dogs (and the students during classes) to suitable areas for training. The dogs are then taken to an area that we have selected for the morning's work. We park the van and walk each of our three dogs for about thirty minutes each.

'We return to the centre mid-morning to change over the dogs and take out the second trip. After a coffee break at Cleve we work the second lot of dogs over the same route as the first trip.

'Shortly before 1 o'clock we go back to the centre and return our load to the kennels.

'At 2.15 everyone is again out in the kennels, loading up vans with dogs and preparing to go out for the afternoon's training. Paul and I have a quick chat about which dogs we shall have and where we shall go.

'The afternoon's work takes much the same form as the morning but we generally park the van in a different place and tackle a slightly different angle of the work. This is particularly so in the latter part of the training when the dogs are more advanced, by which time they will need constant practice at crowd work; shops; traffic and obstacle work. Working in country lanes is also covered, as well as railway and bus stations.

'At 5 o'clock we return to the centre.

'This is, of course, the basic framework of the working day when training dogs, but, as can be imagined, the work is really far more involved than that. Each instructor has between five and seven dogs to train of which four will be used in a class. The reserves will, subsequently, go through another period of three months' training to be used in that instructor's next class. Normally I walk three dogs in each of the morning trips. In the afternoon, those which did not have a walk in the morning come first and then I consider which of the other dogs could benefit from another walk and choose two on that basis, thus making a total of four dogs.

'Each dog is different temperamentally from any other and because of this factor, all dogs must be approached as individuals. Perhaps the wide range of personalities is one of the things which makes the training of the dogs so interesting. No two walks with any dog are ever the same. Even when handed over from the ETU no dog is without its faults, for there is still a lot of work involved in shaping up the basic material and moulding it into a well-trained animal, which it must be by the time it goes into a class. All this must be done in a way whereby the dog enjoys its work because, if it does not enjoy it, it will not ultimately be reliable as a guide dog.'

MILITARY DOGS

Dogs are recognised as being great savers of manpower when used to guard arms depots and installations, and are also wanted for tracking, arms detection and other duties during anti-terrorist operations. It is the responsibility of the Royal Army Veterinary Corps to produce the trained dogs and keep them fit for work, and also to train men to handle them.

Training is carried out at the War Dog Training School and, when qualified, personnel are passed to the following units at home and overseas:

1 RAVC War Dog Training Units—as trainers and instructors for specialist operational dogs and their handlers, ie for tracking, infantry patrol, mine and arms detection.
2 Royal Military Police (RMP) Guard Dog Companies—as trainers and instructors for guard dogs and their handlers. Some military policemen are employed as dog handlers, their training in this aspect being the responsibility of the RAVC.

Promotion within the trade is to Warrant Officer Class II (Chief Instructor) and further progress to Warrant Officer Class I (RSM) is on the corps regimental duty roll. Pay and allowances are at normal army rates (as are pensions) and considered to be most attractive to both married and single men. Further details can be obtained from the Deputy Assistant Director, Army Veterinary Services, the War Office (V&R), Droitwich, Worcs.

POLICE DOGS

This excellent first-hand account of a career as a dog handler in the Police Force has been compiled by Inspector L. Goodall, officer-in-charge of the Hampshire Police Dog Section:

1 People applying to join the Police Force as a dog handler or any other specialised branch of the service are told that in the first instance they must join as a probationary constable and serve for a period of two years. On satisfactory completion of this period they may be considered for a specialist section such as police dogs. The type of officer to be considered must, in addition to the fundamental qualities required in a policeman, show a fondness for animals. It is preferred that he be married with a family and that they all show an equal desire to accept a police dog into the home.

2 Uppermost in a dog handler's mind is the responsibility to care for his dog and, to achieve this, regular exercise and grooming is essential. A dog and its kennel must be kept scrupulously clean to ensure a perfectly healthy animal, fit to carry out the regular and strenuous tasks of police duty. Police dogs are not bred for the purpose but come from perfectly ordinary homes, the owners of which very often find they have bought a young puppy which as it grows becomes too much to handle or expensive to keep, and so it is offered to the police to take over. The acquisition of a new puppy or very young dog immediately becomes a challenge to the police dog handler. The rearing to a specific diet, watching the development of the dog and its temperament are all carefully noted in the initial stages. At ten to

twelve months of age, the real training begins which lasts for thirteen weeks, and is intended to bring the dog and his handler up to a high standard of workmanship and understanding. Each must show understanding, patience, perseverance and dedication. A handler and his dog are trained together in the arts of obedience, agility, tracking and searching. Arresting unarmed and armed criminals is also an important part of the team training. The thirteen weeks of extensive training will soon prove whether or not the selection of the dog handler is correct and whether his dog has the ability and brain to carry out the many tasks asked of him.

3 Although when trained, a police dog lives with his handler and family, he is primarily a one-man animal when it comes to his working hours. Dogs, like human beings, have different temperaments. The purpose of the initial and subsequent training is amongst other things to match these temperaments into a team of complete competence.

4 A police dog and his handler work an eight-hour day and the tasks they are called upon to perform are many and varied. It may be that a young child has failed to return home, and everybody is anxious about his or her safety. It is on these occasions that the dog's training is put to good use in tracking down vital clues. Prisoners may need special escort from one place of detention to another, or a valuable load of property passing through a particular police area may require a special watch kept on it.

5 The dog handler is always in constant radio communication with his station and can be quickly deployed at any time to any part of the county that requires his services. The specially constructed radio control van is a swift means of travel for the handler and his dog. Police dogs are also used for normal patrol work in town centres to check on rowdyism and prevent vandals from destroying valuable property. Many arrests of burglars can be attributed to police dogs who have been put into a building where the intruder is still hiding. It is in such cases that the nose of the dog becomes a valuable aid to the police in crime detection.

6 The police dog handler is a dedicated man to the service, prepared to turn out at all times of the day or night. He and his dog are expected to maintain a high standard of regular training. Each must also be physically fit in order that their specialist requirements can be put to good use at all times.

SHEEPDOGS, GUN DOGS AND HOUNDS

Many diverse breeds of dog fall under this heading. There are few openings here for a career, especially if the person wishing to work with these types of dogs does not come from a country background—where sheep and game birds may be plentiful and, in some cases, the urge to hunt with the hounds has been bred into the bones.

There are no formal schools for training sheepdogs; 99 per cent of the dogs are trained by the farmers themselves and all the offspring come from known working strains. Most of the sheepdogs in England are mongrels, known as curs; in Scotland and Wales they are more likely to be true to a known breed. There is no rule that says a sheep-trials dog has to be a pedigree.

Owners taking part in sheepdog trials and regularly winning contests will seldom sell the dogs' offspring. The prize money is quite high and there is a considerable amount of betting as to the results of each contest, so when an exceptionally good dog shows itself the strain is coveted.

Sheepdog trials are more frequently held in the North of England, Scotland and North Wales than elsewhere in the United Kingdom. A border collie, working with the shepherd to the highest degree of proficiency and intense concentration whilst herding sheep, has a quality that only a shepherd, through his long association and training of the working sheepdog, can fully comprehend.

Gun dogs

In recent years, an increasing number of shoots are being hired by syndicates from farmers. On some marginal agricultural land, a farmer can gain a greater return per acre by stocking a shoot than from farming it in a conventional manner.

There are no centres for training gun dogs in the British Isles. Shooting dogs are trained mostly by keepers or retired keepers, who like to take a dog at eight months old and not older than eleven months, and keep it for a minimum period of three months. An average weekly charge for training a gun dog in 1973 was £5.00, including food. One veterinary surgeon, with two very good spaniel bitches to breed from, manages to train three gun dogs a year. Such is the reputation he has acquired over a five-year period that he has a waiting list of two years; he is able to sell the trained dogs for £140 each, the surplus untrained puppies fetching between £20 and £25 each. As a sideline, training gun dogs can prove to be both interesting and remunerative.

There is no such thing as a good all-round shooting dog. There are different breeds for different jobs: labradors for open country—finding, retrieving and particularly for water work; spaniels for hedgerows, roots and heavy undergrowth—their thick coats protect them from brambles and thorns. Pointers and setters are trained to point within 10–15yd of a hidden bird and will stay rigid until the bird has moved away; dogs which have attained this high standard and prove to be reliable are usually over three years old.

It is seldom that a puppy from a non-working strain will make a satisfactory gun dog, however good the training; therefore when buying a puppy it is important to know as much as possible about its background. When acquiring a gun dog purely for shooting, it is essential, prior to purchase, to secure a veterinary certificate of immunity from progressive retinal atrophy—a hereditary eye disease which can be determined by an experienced veterinary surgeon in the parents of a puppy, providing the former are over two years old. This disease appears to be more prevalent in the South of England and is chiefly confined to labradors, retrievers and spaniels. There is no real cure for this disease, and the dog begins to go blind soon after the age of three.

Most dogs learn more from other well-trained dogs than by any other means. A badly trained dog can spoil a shoot. A trained dog should not wear a collar when working; a young untrained dog is best on a choke chain—it will learn more quickly not to be head strong with this type of restraint. About one in every hundred gun dogs is gun shy—which is incurable. Gun dogs are trained to work from side to side, never forwards to backwards; this is known as quartering. Whilst working out in the field, whether in stubble, roots, grass or even plough, the dogs are never more than 20yd in front of the guns. When a standing gun has a dog with him, it is trained to sit about 2yd in front of him, never behind.

Mr Jack Craven, a well-known sportsman from the West Riding of Yorkshire, considers that the ideal combination of gun dogs is to have a labrador and a spaniel working together.

There is a considerable difference between a dog trained for field-trial competitions and one trained for shooting. Whilst many people may use them for both, it is seldom satisfactory. A field-trial dog is trained to stay close to its master and *not* to hunt but only to find and retrieve. If it is to be any good at winning prizes it has to be absolutely rock steady, so it is trained not to show any initiative as it must hear the appropriate sounds for 'Wait', no matter what it is doing.

No gun dog can become a show champion, however many challenge certificates it has won, unless it has received a qualifying certificate at a field-trial meeting. The importance of this ruling being that, before the gun dog can receive a prize, it must display certain natural attributes.

Hounds

The merits of hunting with hounds scarcely comes within the scope of this book. The familiar argument of the keen fox hunter that if foxes were not preserved for hunting they would all be shot and poisoned by the farmers has a sound basis. Hunting foxes as a renewable resource, to say the least, helps to guarantee their survival. Records from the famous Yorkshire pack, the Braham Moor, show that between 1877 and 1908, 3,302 foxes were killed. As foxes are still prolific in the same areas today, the Braham Moor hunt could, ironically, claim to be the fox's guardian.

Water pollution is taking such a heavy toll of the dwindling otter population of the British Isles that it is hoped the hunting of this animal will come to a halt, before the otter completely disappears from our waterways.

GREYHOUNDS

The future for greyhound racing is not as promising as it was just after the last war when, in the late 1940s, there were fifteen stadiums in the London area alone; now there are only half that number. However, in spite of a declining interest in greyhound racing, it is still a sizeable industry employing a good number of people.

The National Greyhound Racing Association and Property Trust is the largest greyhound racing concern in Britain, owning the majority of the larger stadiums including the White City, Harringay, Clacton and Wembley. The association's 140-acre headquarters is at the Hook Kennels near Potters Bar in Hertfordshire, where thirty or so kennelmaids are employed to look after some 650 greyhounds.

The majority of the kennel staff are recruited during the local school career conventions. A girl can be employed as a kennelmaid on leaving school at the age of sixteen. Living at the kennels is compulsory for junior staff; parents of school leavers are interviewed and must give written permission for their daughters to live away from home. No previous experience with animal work is required, and no qualifying period is involved. For anyone keen and alert, the work can be extremely interesting.

Promotion is naturally based on ability but, as this is not an expanding industry, senior post vacancies are limited. There are fourteen to fifteen trainers at the kennels, each with a staff of one head kennel lad or girl, and two or three kennelmaids. The head lad or girl is responsible for the trainer's kennel in his absence. It is possible for a kennel lad or girl to achieve a trainer's rating after five to ten years' service.

Pay rates are laid down by the association, female staff being paid the same as the men. A rise can be expected after the initial three months and then at regular yearly intervals.

Working hours are elastic. A normal day is from 8 am to 4.30 pm; on race days, which occur twice a week throughout the year, evening work is usually between 8 pm and 10.30 pm. Three weeks' paid leave is given after one year, and four weeks after five years.

CHAPTER TWO
Cats

BOARDING CATTERIES

My experience with cats has chiefly revolved round the so-called 'wild' species—cheetah, serval and lion. All of these I first encountered in Africa; two of them I have had as pets, trusting them as much as any domestic cat. Chinky, a three-and-a-half-year-old lioness who used to wash my face with her sandpaper-like tongue, taught me a great deal about the true understanding of animal friendship and mutual respect. Although one is unlikely to encounter any of these species at a boarding cattery, the work involved in seeing to their daily welfare cannot be entirely dissimilar. For all cats, whether large or small, will condescendingly respond to humans and, while doing so, still maintain their dignity and independence.

Anyone contemplating working with cats must realise from the outset that love is not enough. Cats as a species are enchanting creatures, but every one is an individual and, when boarded for the first time, some can be very difficult indeed. Whilst the work is in many ways rewarding—though not financially so—it is mostly hard, unremitting toil, calling for endless patience, vigilance and utter reliability. Delightful though cats may be, caring for them often lacks glamour. The cat which has persistent diarrhoea, from whatever cause, and seems incapable of recognising a litter tray, can prove both tiresome and time consuming. Equally worrying is the one who steadfastly refuses to eat; having established that there is nothing wrong with the cat, only patience will win the day. Anyone with a genuine sympathy and understanding of animals will realise that the cat cannot help it and must be dealt with gently.

To embark on a career in connection with boarding catteries, the following can be considered:

1 To own and operate a boarding cattery. Land, capital and planning permission are required. This is no gold-mine financially and is better described as a small treadmill.
2 To work as an assistant in a boarding cattery. This help is much in demand but not particularly well paid. It is, however, a job calling for utter reliability, endless patience and a sympathetic understanding of animals.
3 The post of manager or manageress of a boarding cattery. This may include living accommodation plus a salary.

The Feline Advisory Bureau compiles a list of approved boarding catteries, which are awarded a star rating by the Bureau Council in recognition of their professional standing. The Bureau was founded in 1958 with two main objects:

Generally to promote humane behaviour towards the cat and to assure its physical and mental wellbeing by giving advice to owners on its maintenance in health and care in sickness;
To establish such special funds as may be thought desirable to promote investigations into feline diseases.

In my search for a high-standard star-rated boarding establishment, I chose the Stonehenge Cats' Hotel near Salisbury in Wiltshire. Miss Hamilton Moore, the proprietor, is well equipped to provide a first-hand appraisal of the nature of working with cats as well as its responsibilities. Her observations on cat boarding are as follows:

The immense responsibility of operating a boarding cattery is not always fully appreciated either by the public or, regrettably, by some cattery proprietors and employees. There is a great demand for boarding catteries; anyone contemplating starting one should consult the Feline Advisory Bureau, which runs a Boarding Cattery Information Service providing specifications and an excellent layout drawn up in consultation with the British Small Animals Veterinary Association. However, a good boarding cattery does not depend solely upon the excellence of its buildings, which will be totally useless unless the husbandry and hygiene are meticulous and the administration sound and efficient. Over and above this, if at all possible, the surroundings should be pleasant and well kept, with trees and bushes that attract wild birds and butterflies, thus giving the cats plenty to watch, so combating boredom. Geese, ducks and ornamental waterfowl or any animals other than dogs will always stimulate their interest.

Administration must be not only efficient but must be seen to be efficient. An anxious owner will be greatly reassured by the attention paid to an individual cat's requirements. For this purpose every cat should be given a record card. The owner should sign an authorisation for veterinary treatment and produce the cat's up-to-date certificate of vaccination against feline enteritis. No cattery should ever accept an uninoculated cat. On departure, the owner should sign a release form to the effect that the cat is in good health and should settle the account.

It is the proud boast of some establishments that they are the biggest in the area and can accommodate 60, 80 or 100 cats. This is in fact no recommendation, indeed rather the reverse. Broadly speaking, two people can give the vitally necessary individual attention to 25–30 cats but certainly no more. Ideally a husband-and-wife team, or two sisters or partners, plus one part- or full-time assistant form an adequate work force for anything up to forty cats, *but no more*. There is more to working in a cattery than cleaning and feeding. Supplies must be obtained and ordered, accounts kept, buildings and garden maintained, chalets kept in good repair, and every cat carefully studied and watched.

The Stonehenge Cats' Hotel has twenty chalets, 4ft by 4ft by 6ft, insulated, lined, sealed and painted; with infra-red heating; and concrete runs 6ft by 4ft by 6ft with scratching posts, and 2ft between runs. Facilities include numbered equipment; disposable beds and feeding dishes; safety passage; isolation unit, and cats' kitchen. Very strict attention is paid to hygiene; inoculated cats only being accepted.

A typical day's work at this cat hotel is as follows:

Between 7 and 8 am all the buildings are unlocked and the hot water is switched on. The cat doors of all the occupied chalets are opened, and the heating is either switched off or adjusted, according to the weather. The condition of each cat is checked while the drinking dishes and food plates are being collected.

The drinking dishes are then washed with a non-toxic disinfectant, and meals are prepared according to individual menus. Each owner completes a record card when registering the cat as a border. Questions concerning the animal's culinary whims include: Does your cat like rabbit, fish, cooked meat, raw meat, milk, tinned food (please name variety)? Is there any food that must be avoided? If only some human hotels could be as discerning!

Each chalet is washed out with a disinfectant/detergent solution. The litter trays are cleaned and renewed, and the runs and the safety passages swept. When this is completed, the cats are fed and given fresh milk and water. Solid litter, disposable plates and bedding, and all combustible rubbish is incinerated. A note is made of any cats suffering from constipation or diarrhoea, or which has failed to urinate or eat, or has been drinking excessively, has vomited, or whose condition is in any way questionable. If a health problem does present itself, the decision is taken whether or not to call in a veterinary surgeon. At this stage of the morning, any cat requiring medication or treatment is dealt with.

Any recently vacated chalets are disinfected. This involves clearing the run of the scratching post and wooden box on which the cat sits. The entire chalet is scrubbed out and dried. The wooden bearers, wire netting and interior of the chalet are then pressure-sprayed with a 1 per cent solution of disinfectant. The interior is wiped with a clean disposable cloth, and fresh bed, litter tray and sweeping brush are put in for the next occupant. The scratching post and wooden box are heavily drenched with disinfectant. The run is pressure-hosed and scrubbed. The scratching post and box are replaced and a 1 per cent solution of disinfectant poured liberally over the entire surface of the run and allowed to dry. Used litter trays are scrubbed with detergent, thoroughly rinsed and dried, then sprayed with disinfectant and allowed to dry before being put away.

Grooming is carried out during the morning, with particular attention to long-haired cats and, especially in high summer, much time is spent treating cats for fleas.

Whilst this is going on, the telephone will ring constantly, owners will arrive to deposit or collect cats, and countless other interruptions will occur. As time permits, the menu must be compiled for the evening meal and the following day's breakfast. Towards the end of the morning, the evening meal must be prepared.

Miss Hamilton Moore always endeavours to get the bulk of the work done in the morning, partly in order to leave the cats in peace for an hour or two in the afternoon, and partly to give herself some time for dealing with paperwork, the ordering of food and supplies, and looking after the garden.

The cats are fed again at 4 or 5 pm, depending on the time of year. Litter trays are attended to and each cat's condition is noted. Before dusk, according to the temperature and weather conditions, the cats are shut into their chalets, for they are not allowed the freedom of their run at night.

Each cat is visited last thing at night and any cleaning up is done. Heating is switched on and thermostats adjusted.

PEDIGREE CAT BREEDING

There are some thirty-three species of domestic cat recognised by the Governing Council of the Cat Fancy. The majority of these species each has a breed society affiliated to the Governing Council. In order to sell kittens as pedigree stock, the breeder has to be registered with either the Short-haired Registrar, or the Long-haired Registrar, according to which group the cat belongs.

Mrs Francesca Roden has been successfully breeding chinchilla, smoke and black long-hairs for over ten years and has also become a well-known judge of these breeds. Here is her advice on taking up pedigree cat breeding as a career:

As a rule, the majority of cat breeding establishments are run by a single person, as very few are large or lucrative enough to employ staff. In general, it is best that this is so, as cats are very individual in character, and blossom when treated with continuity of care, with the same pair of careful hands and observant eyes to notice details, and to feel responsibility. A constant watch must be kept in the various stages of reproduction, as well as noticing changes in health, when in season, among other things; and a cat's character develops more fully when in close contact with the owner.

It is difficult to say how many cats should be kept on average, since it depends entirely on the amount of time any one person can devote to them. Two breeding queens (brood females) could, with careful thought and organisation, be undertaken as an extra to other activities, bearing in mind that at certain periods—such as mating, kittening and weaning—much extra time will be required. Three and upwards would be more of a full-time occupation in the breeding season, since there is much to do in the way of organising food supplies and preparation of meals, and the cleaning and maintenance of accommodation and runs. If a stud cat (an entire male) is kept, which is another branch of cat breeding, visiting queens must be accommodated and matings supervised; there will be an extra boarder to look after if a queen stays several days. There will be visits from those interested in buying a kitten; another of the breeder's responsibilities is to ascertain that good care and a suitable environment is in store for it.

The queen decides when she shall have a family; this means that it cannot be organised in advance, except for an approximate date. It is essential for the owner to be on hand at these times to ascertain that all is going well, to give aid if necessary and to impart confidence. If there is this dedication to sustain, the delights are many. Feline companionship is subtle and rewarding when there is a close bond, and there is the joy of watching kittens develop and progress to the enchanting stage of playing and learning about life, and the gratification of having been the mainspring which brought this beauty and movement into existence. There is the excitement, too, of welcoming each family, and of waiting to see, as they grow, whether the new little ones have made the step forward envisaged and hoped for.

An essential part of serious breeding is attending and exhibiting at cat shows. This means extra special daily grooming for at least a week prior to the show, and entails a very early start to the day or travelling overnight. It is important to enter competitions so as to assess whether the breeding is progressing on the right lines. To win at a show gives a glow of achievement which lightens the daily routine.

The day starts with the clearing, washing and replenishing of overnight toilet trays, followed by breakfast, then the cleaning of the cats' accommodation. All cats should be groomed daily, including eyes and ears as well as coats, which on some days may need the extra attention of the application of powder and brushing out. With only a few cats to groom, this may be accomplished in the morning; with more residents, it has to be fitted in later in the day. The mid-day meal is one of the highspots, with a last meal at night, and 'tea' in between. Expectant mothers and nursing queens require an extra meal, as do newly weaned kittens. Rearing kittens takes more time—teaching them to lap, cutting meat minutely for small stomachs in the early stages of growth, and clearing toilet trays several times a day to keep the kittens clean and well trained. The little ones should also be groomed every day, so that they accept this procedure as a matter of course. Much commonsense is required, such as parting the kittens from their mother for a while before each meal during weaning, so that they will be hungry enough to take food from a human, and will start learning to be independent.

There is seldom a typical day for a cat breeder. There may be show preparation; a queen to be taken for mating to the chosen sire when she is in season, and this might be some distance away; kittens to wean, or an appointment for a visitor. Paperwork involves form filling for entering a show, registering kittens, writing pedigrees and answering inquiries. It is so diverse that there is always interest. One is continually learning when there is the enthusiasm to take up the challenge which this fascinating subject presents, and it is very fulfilling.

If the initial interest is there, it is suggested that several championship cat shows be attended in order to observe the many varieties of pedigree cats and decide which has the most appeal. The long-hairs (Persians) need more time spent on their coats than the short-haired varieties, and it is better not to specialise in more than one or two kinds. Going to a show will give some idea of what is involved in breeding pedigree cats, and there will be the opportunity of speaking to experienced breeders and seeing how to go about taking the first steps. Borrowing books on cats from the local library is recommended; reading about the subject is most valuable in acquiring some groundwork and in learning about the various breeds.

The main requirements—given the right conditions for breeding cats—are patience, for success does not come overnight; consideration, which means having the ability to look at things from the feline point of view; being observant and prepared to take trouble, and all topped up with good common sense.

It usually takes several years and considerable financial outlay before a successful strain is established, when the fruits of endeavour show in the progeny being prized and sought after. The intervening time is spent in patiently building a line by learning about pedigree, observing good examples, developing expertise and finding flair for this rewarding subject—rewarding in the sense of satisfaction derived from success in improving and bringing to realisation the standard laid down, plus the knowledge that a contribution is being made in furthering the beauty of a healthy strain.

RESEARCH ESTABLISHMENTS

Another opportunity of working with cats is available at research establishments, where candidates are likely to further their career if they first of all qualify as a Registered Animal Nursing Auxiliary (see Chapter 7). Female workers are preferred for the majority of posts in this field. Although certainly not the type of work to attract the emotional cat lover, scientific research is obviously necessary for the health and welfare of domestic cats in general.

As a rewarding career in animal management—offering experience in the maintenance, breeding and basic medication of cats—it can be recommended for the more technician-minded candidate.

CHAPTER THREE

Horses

I first sat on a horse at the age of three; fell off a horse at three and a half, and started to learn to ride seriously when I was six.

Like many young horse enthusiasts, I was weaned on Anna Sewell's classic *Black Beauty* and consequently regarded all black horses as paragons of virtue and thought all chestnuts were as temperamental as Ginger. Regrettably, I did not have much opportunity to continue riding until my regular army days in the Federation of Rhodesia and Nyasaland's Staff Corps, when I spent many an enjoyable hour trekking through the African bush on horseback. Having enjoyed a good deal of riding during my childhood, I look back to that time with great nostalgia, thinking how satisfactory it would be to be permanently involved with horses.

TRAINING AND QUALIFICATIONS

For young people wishing to make their career with horses the best advice is provided by Colonel Nigel Grove-White, Training and Development Officer of the British Horse Society:

(a) They should complete their general education as far as possible and not cut short their time at school. Indeed, the first examinations of the ability to teach riding can only be attempted at the age of seventeen and a half. Candidates for the BHS assistant instructor's examination will normally be expected to hold two GCE 'O' level certificates (one in English language or literature) or equivalent; and a valid British Red Cross or St John Ambulance initial first aid certificate or equivalent.

These requirements will not apply to those opting for the horsemaster's certificate only—which is the BHS assistant instructor's examination without instructional element.

(b) They should aim at acquiring as good a basic training as possible in riding and horse-management. The best riding schools provide a sound training in their horsemastership and working pupil's courses. These courses, which last three–fifteen months, are designed to prepare adults or school leavers for the BHS assistant instructor's examination, and for the horsemaster's examination.

The BHS publishes a list of approved riding establishments showing the facilities available. This information is helpful in selecting a school most suitable for individual requirements. Those interested can write direct to the schools listed for details of courses and fees. The standard of instruction can be gauged by the qualifications of the instructors. It is recommended that a personal visit is arranged to an establishment before a final decision is made.

Colonel Grove-White makes a point of mentioning that education authorities have the power to allocate grants to school leavers who wish to become riding instructors. The allocation of a grant is entirely at the discretion of the individual local authority; unfortunately not all education authorities will give such aid to potential riding instructors, but it is always worth trying. Applications should be made to the educational officer of the local authority, preferably some months before leaving school.

The BHS publishes a pamphlet giving detailed information about training and qualifications, as follows:

A thorough basic training is essential for the young person who intends taking up a career with horses just as for any other profession. That they can ride, have won a few prizes in competitions and can't think of anything else to do to earn a living is not sufficient preparation for a lifelong occupation. Yet many enter the profession with no more qualifications than this and even set up as teachers, running their own 'schools'.

The recognised qualifications in the world of horses in Britain are the certificates awarded by the British Horse Society. There are three levels of certificate for instructors—the assistant instructor's (BHSAI), the instructor's (BHSI) and the fellowship (FBHS); and two levels for stable managers—the BHS horsemaster and the BHS stable manager. These certificates are essential to any young person setting out to work with horses as a life-time's occupation. The scope of the examination syllabus is such that the possession of the BHSI or the fellowship will be sufficient qualification for almost any position with horses, with the possible exception of stud work. That there are many excellent though technically unqualified people working successfully in all branches of the horse world is no reason for neglecting to acquire qualifications. Most of these people were setting out on their careers before the examinations were brought into being and have become 'qualified' by long experience. As a new entrant, it is foolish to be placed at a disadvantage at the outset of a career by not obtaining qualifications.

To have a reasonable chance of passing the BHS exams, it will be necessary to attend a good riding school, preferably as a resident pupil. Choose a school with qualified instructors, recommended by the BHS in their List of Approved Riding Establishments. Note that BHSAI, BHSI and FBHS are the only letters which signify an instructor qualified under the Society's scheme (also BHS Prelim, as BHSAI was formerly known). The letters MBHS, often seen displayed outside a school, mean no more than that the proprietor has, at some time, paid a subscription and joined the Society, but this is in no way a qualification.

The only other recognised teaching qualifications are the IIH (Instructor of the Institute of the Horse) and FIH (Fellowship of the Institute). These were awarded prior to the inception of the BHS.

To illustrate the type of work in which candidates are likely to involve themselves before qualifying for the assistant instructor's certificate, the following is quoted from the syllabus of the examination:

Equitation

Correct position and use of aids at all paces
Turns and circles at all paces
Transitions from one pace to another
Rein back
Jumping a course of small fences out of a trot and canter, up to approx 3ft 3in and to include a double
Riding without stirrups

Stable management and horsemanship

STABLE ROUTINE including:
(a) Daily routine
(b) Organisation of a yard as regards feeding, bedding, droppings, watering, sweeping
(c) Organisation of tack room
(d) Grooming kit
(e) Clothing

ELEMENTARY SHOEING including:
Reasons for shoeing; how a shoe should fit; conformation of foot
Reasons for special shoeing
How to remove a shoe

CLIPPING, TRIMMING AND PLAITING including:
Kind of machine in every day use; types of clip

How to pull a mane and tail
How to plait a mane and tail
Singeing

CARE OF THE HORSE IN THE OPEN including:
Preparing a horse to be turned out, and getting the horse up
Supervision of horse's health, feet, watering, shelter
Protection of wounds and sores

CARE OF THE HORSE IN STABLES including:
Exercise and work; grooming and quartering; rugging up and bandaging; preparing horse for a journey

FITTING OF SADDLERY including:
Precautions against sore backs and girth galls
Simple questions on bits, their fittings and uses

Minor ailments (written)
How to take a temperature and pulse
How to suspect temperature
How to drench and ball
How to deal with infection and contagion
How to dress wounds—punctures, clean cuts or contusions
How to deal with excessive bleeding
How to recognise and deal with colic
How to deal with fevers, colds and coughs
How to recognise lameness
How to recognise obvious unsoundness of limbs, feet and wind
How to treat galls, sprains, etc
How to treat foment, tub, hose or poultice
When to call in a veterinary surgeon

Powers of instruction
Giving a simple lesson to show:

Knowledge of the principles of instruction
Voice and manner
Control of ride
Demonstration

Once the first certificates are achieved—BHS assistant instructor's for potential instructors and BHS horsemaster's for stable managers—and thereby a basic training on sound lines, then good employment is easily found in schools or private stables, where the all-important experience can be gained.

RIDING STABLES

Mr and Mrs F. B. Finnis own the Louanne Riding Centre at St Peter, Jersey, where they stable some forty-five horses. Mick Finnis has been directly involved with horses for some twenty years. In 1958, whilst serving in the army, he attended an equitation course at the Royal Army Veterinary Corps Training Centre at Melton Mowbray. Later he became for five years British pentathlon champion—running, shooting, swimming, fencing and riding—representing Great Britain at the 1964 Olympic Games in Tokyo. Angela Finnis, who founded the Louanne Riding Centre, qualified as a riding instructor in the early 1960s.

This husband-and-wife team run a highly professional average-sized riding establishment. They own twenty of the horses, the remainder being kept, exercised and fed at the stables for various owners. This livery service provides the riding centre with a regular 'bread and butter' income. The Finnises are assisted by two stablemen and three stable girls.

Over 80 per cent of the riding centre's young clientele are female, while for an ever-increasing number of men and women between the ages of thirty-two and sixty riding has become a favourite pastime.

Mick and Angela Finnis insist on a rest day for all the horses every Monday. Especially during the busy times of the year, a great deal of riding is done by all concerned—apart from lessons, preparation goes on for gymkhanas and other competitions. Health problems naturally present themselves from time to time, when veterinary advice must be sought and medication becomes necessary. Each horse has to be re-shod every month at a local forge. All this takes up a lot of time.

The basic working hours for the staff are from 07.00 to 18.00 hours, six days a week, with a two-week paid holiday. Wages are arranged by private negotiation. The pattern of daily work at the stables is as follows:

07.00 All the horses are checked before the mucking out of the loose boxes commences. Once the wood shavings and the hay have been replenished, food and fresh water are provided. The daily rations consist of—amongst other foodstuffs—bran, oats, barley, horse nuts, beet pulp, hay and cod liver oil.

09.00 The outside stable yards are swept and hosed down. In preparation for the first riding lesson of the day, each mount is groomed and saddled.

10.30 The first riding lesson is taken by either Mick or Angela Finnis, or both of them together. An average of ten to twelve horses are taken out at each lesson, which lasts for approximately one hour. In the summer a class of up to twenty riders may necessitate four instructors being on hand to cope with leading reins and any emergencies that present themselves. During busy periods, there are normally four lessons a day. When the horses are returned to their loose boxes, the stable staff remove the harness, and each horse is carefully rubbed down. Those horses that are not being used in the morning or afternoon lessons are groomed and exercised by the stable girls in the morning.

12.15 All the hay nets are taken to the loft and filled with approximately 26lb of hay.

14.00 During busy times of the year, the afternoon hourly lessons are given between 14.30 and 16.30, and the stable staff must have the required number of horses ready at the specified time. When jumping tuition is the order of the day, the mounts are warmed up during the first half of the lesson; then for the remaining half-hour the riders take the horses over the various jumps, whose height and structure depend on the riders' experience and ability.

14.45 Whilst the lessons are in progress, the stable girls see to the maintenance and cleaning of the tack and grooming equipment.

18.00 A normal working day finishes at this time, but not before all the needs of the horses have been catered for. Those that have been ridden in the afternoon are rubbed down. All the horses are fed and watered, as they are not seen to again for over thirteen hours.

Anyone embarking on a career at a riding school must be prepared for all aspects of the work—mucking out, cleaning tack, grooming, exercising, or instructing. A basic enthusiasm for the job will compensate for any lack of financial reward, for pay is adequate rather than handsome.

HUNTING STABLES

Hunting and racing provide the greatest volume of employment in the horse world. The BHS pamphlet, *A Career with Horses*, states that more and more hunt stables employ girl grooms; this is seasonal employment, few staff being kept through the summer. There is no opportunity for a career in hunt service for girls, but for young men wishing to become hunt servants—eventually to carry the horn as professional huntsmen—the best approach is via the stables, working up from strapper to second horseman, to second whipper-in, to whip, until the goal is reached. It is advisable to choose a well-established pack having a continuity of mastership and therefore security of employment.

Hunting also gives opportunities for employment in private stables.

RACING STABLES

The bulk of the work in connection with racing stables is done by males. Jump jockeys are frequently flat-racing jockeys who have become too heavy for steeplechasing. A school leaver weighing between 5½ and 6 stone, and ambitious to become a first-class jockey, might consider flat racing as a career.

Mrs Susan Elsie, wife of the well-known Yorkshire trainer, Bill Elsie, has contributed the following information:

Apprentices go to the stables as school leavers and sign a document of intentment for a period of between three and seven years (although they are always released from the terms set down in the document if they do not like the life or they become too heavy). No academic qualifications are required, although all good jockeys are intelligent people. Apprentices should weigh about 5½–6 stone when they arrive as school leavers, otherwise they are too heavy when they start riding in races. Boys do not need previous experience with horses, but it does help if they have ridden ponies prior to engagement.

The apprentice starts off in the stable doing odd jobs, helping with the cleaning and feeding, under the instruction of one of the experienced lads. After this, he will be given two or three horses to look after and the daily routine will involve:

06.00 Muck out two or three horses and dress over (groom).
06.45 Exercise first horse, walk, trot, canter and—some days—work (gallop).
07.30 Return first horse to stable, dress over, provide with hay and water.
08.00 Ride second horse (same as for first horse).
09.00 Return second horse to stable (and see to as for first). Tea break.
10.30 Ride third horse (same as for first and second).
12.00 Feed all three horses. Time free until 16.00.
16.00 Muck out, dress over ready for inspection by trainer.
18.00 Hay, water and final feed of the day.

When a boy's horse is ready to race he will accompany it to the races (lead up). If the race course is some distance away he will have to stay overnight and it is his responsibility to look after his horse in the same way as he does at home (under supervision of travelling head lad): dress over, lead round the paddock prior to the race; after the race, wash down, dry off and dress over.

In his second or third year, depending on the ability he shows on the home gallops, the apprentice will be given some rides in public. If he rides well—ie follows the trainer's instructions and possibly even wins or is placed—other trainers may give him rides. If he continues well, he is on the way to being a jockey, though comparatively few get this far. For those who are less successful, or who get too heavy (the lowest weight a horse carries is 7 stone, but an apprentice can claim up to 7lb—ie rides at 6 stone 7lb), the life and work in stables may satisfy them until they retire.

For every lad who becomes a jockey of renown, experiencing the glamour and excitement of the profession, there are hundreds who never get as far as riding exercise. As a career, the prospects for girls are almost nil and only the really outstanding boys have a chance of making the grade.

POLO PONIES, SHOW HORSES AND TREKKING CENTRES

For those in search of summer work, there are opportunities in looking after polo ponies, show horses and show jumpers, and at trekking centres.

Polo is played at various centres, where the grooms, privately employed, are usually based with their ponies. The job of looking after polo ponies is most suitable for the younger girl, as the work is not so arduous as with hunters.

Show horses, which can include harness horses, also provide suitable work for a young girl. This will entail much travelling and some 'living rough'. Many owners employ professional riders to show their horses, some retaining their services throughout the winter. With show jumpers, there will be fewer opportunities to ride, other than exercising, as not many owners employ professional riders.

Trekking centres are now an established part of the horse world. Grooms, guides and leaders enjoy a fair amount of riding amid lovely scenery, although the majority of jobs concerned with this popular holiday trend are only seasonal. For those interested in trekking, full details can be obtained from the governing body for trekking centres in the British Isles: Ponies of Britain, Brookside Farm, Winkfield Row, Ascot, Berkshire.

STUDS AND BREEDING

For those to whom riding is not the main attraction, but rather the care of animals, work in studs or breeding centres can bring great satisfaction. There are openings for both sexes, although female personnel are usually employed with brood mares, so that they can look after them during foaling.

Owing to the greatly increased demand for well-qualified staff, salaries are now comparable to those of other careers; in addition there are such perquisites as continued training and possible competition riding, while residence and board are necessarily included as animals must be continually attended. Tax relief may be obtained for the special clothing required.

POLICE HORSES

The Metropolitan Police Mounted Branch have long supplied one of the colourful sights of London, and do much to further a happy relationship between the police and the public.

Chief Superintendent A. L. Pilden describes the background, training and duties of London's mounted police:

In all probability, the Mounted Branch is the oldest section of the Metropolitan Force. At the beginning of the last century, each man carried a sabre, pistol, truncheon and a pair of handcuffs; they were clothed in scarlet waistcoats (giving rise to their nickname of 'Redbreasts'), blue greatcoats and trousers, black leather hats and stocks, white leather gloves and steel-spurred boots. This was the first uniform to be issued to any police force, and although small in number, they proved, in an age when the horses stood supreme, that their service to the community was invaluable.

The Mounted Branch today consists of some 200 horses and 210 men, and is still under the control of an assistant commissioner, with a chief superintendent in direct command. The branch is divided into four areas, as is the force as a whole, with a superintendent or chief inspector in charge of each area. The distribution of the branch throughout the Metropolitan Police District is governed by the need for mounted patrols in particular areas, and is frequently reviewed in the light of changing circumstances.

Before being considered for entry into the Mounted Branch, an officer must complete two years' ordinary or 'foot' duty to ensure that he is well-grounded in general police work before specialising as a mounted officer.

In earlier days, many applicants were former cavalry or horse artillery men, but today the majority of recruits have no previous experience. After preliminary interview and test to determine his suitability, each successful applicant receives a twenty-two-week course at Imber Court, where he is taught grooming, riding, handling and general care of horses and saddlery.

This is a preliminary training course in horsemanship and horsemastership, in addition to which every sergeant and constable with less than twenty-five years' service will have to attend an annual refresher course to maintain his efficiency and ability. At the end of the twenty-two-week course, an officer is posted to one of the larger stables as 'mounted reserve' (ie without a horse); he thus gains further experience by riding horses on patrol that are allocated to men absent due to sickness, leave, etc. This posting is normally for a period of about six months, at the end of which he becomes permanently established and is allocated his own horse.

Mounted police officers from many overseas countries and provincial forces attend Imber Court for both primary and advanced training courses.

Whilst the majority of police horses are purchased in Yorkshire, where the requirements are well known to farmers and breeders, some are purchased from other sources and occasionally a gift horse is received. Only mares or geldings are purchased, ideally three or four years old, 16 hands high, of good general colour, ie black, brown, chestnut, bay or grey. A half- to three-quarter-bred animal is well suited to police work. This breeding combines all the admirable qualities of the thoroughbred horse with the strength and substance of the draught animal—the greatest part of the police horse's working life being carried out on the hard roads.

The horse's training is designed to produce a quiet, well-mannered animal that is well-balanced, obedient to the correct 'aids', accustomed to moving traffic of ever-increasing speed and volume, and to unusual sights and sounds, and that will work equally well alone and in the company of other horses. Whilst the average horse takes about six months to train, there are no hard and fast rules since each animal has to be treated as an individual, according to age, breeding, temperament, condition and conformation. Their training is entrusted to police officers selected for their ability in this field, each normally having two horses under training at one time.

However tractable a horse may be, its training is never hurried; the best guide to the experienced trainer being the reactions of the individual animal. The training period can be divided into three stages; the first covers handling, lungeing and driving, ie work carried out from the ground with the object of preparing the horse both physically and mentally for the subsequent stages. The second stage is carried out from the saddle after the horse has been 'backed', the object being gradually to acquire complete control over its mental and physical powers and to accustom it to the conditions under which its duties will eventually be performed. Preliminary work with flags, rattles, music, etc, in preparation for ceremonial duties, also takes place.

Sound reproduction facilities in the form of a tape recorder and amplifying equipment are used in the covered riding school to simulate various background noises, such as railway trains, football crowds, ceremonial occasions and even a jet aircraft at close quarters. This familiarisation with unusual sights and sounds is carried out over a period, as is all training, commencing in the closed school and progressing to the open.

Training in crowd control is carried out by teaching the horses to move laterally (pass) into groups of people, this having been found to be the safest and most efficient method. During all this training, the greatest care is taken not to over-face or frighten the horse, the whole system being based on encouragement and reward.

The results of this training can be seen at the Metropolitan Police Horse Show and Tournament held annually at Imber Court, East Molesey, Surrey, generally on the last Friday and Saturday of July.

At the completion of this initial training, the horse is allocated to a suitable mounted officer of experience and ability, who is responsible for the animal's final training on the street and in the various duties comprising the working life of a police horse. Great care is exercised in matching horse and rider to ensure a suitable partnership in which mutual confidence and understanding can be established and maintained.

On a normal day, a mounted officer patrols for three hours, the rest of his eight-hour tour of duty being spent grooming (before and after patrol), general stable work, cleaning tack etc. He is posted to a patrol and, in working it, has the same responsibilities as his 'foot' colleagues, with the added advantage of being at such a height from the ground that he can see into enclosed yards and premises, and can use his powers of observation to a much greater extent than his mobile colleague who is obliged to keep his eyes on the road! He assists with general traffic control, deals with crime, rowdyism, traffic and other offences, and, of course, continually answers questions from the public.

The duty at which the Mounted Branch excels is the control of crowds—at a ceremonial occasion, a big sporting event, such as a football match or a race meeting, or a demonstration. It has been said that on such occasions a trained man on a trained horse can do the work of a dozen police officers on foot. The value of a mounted officer is the fact that he has a great psychological advantage over a large crowd and is able to see over the heads to pinpoint areas of pressure or trouble, and if necessary take the appropriate action. He is thus able to prevent the development of difficult or dangerous situations.

Looking back over the history of the mounted police of London, and considering the uses to which the police horse is put even in this technological age, it is difficult to imagine any time in the future when the combination of man and horse will not have a useful function to perform as an integral part of the Metropolitan Police.

Anyone wishing to take up this interesting and comparatively well-paid career should write for further details to the Chief Superintendent, Metropolitan Mounted Police Training Establishment, Imber Court, East Molesey, Surrey.

MILITARY HORSES

Household Cavalry

The world-famous Household Cavalry Mounted Regiment consists of one Life Guards mounted squadron and one Blues and Royals mounted squadron. The regiment is quartered at Knightsbridge, London, in modern attractive barracks. The skyscraper that houses the soldiers' families has one of the finest views overlooking Hyde Park.

If mounted duty is chosen, the recruit will go to the Mounted Regiment in London for an intensive twenty-two-week riding course, at the end of which he can take his place in The Queen's Life Guard or in a Sovereign's Escort. All soldiers on mounted duty are volunteers. They are taught to ride and jump and look after their horses. There are also opportunities to learn a specialist trade, such as blacksmith, tailor and saddler.

After a tour of three years with horses in Knightsbridge, a soldier normally does his armoured training in either tanks or armoured cars. Those who start their army life on the armoured side may, if they wish, go to Knightsbridge for a tour of mounted duty.

Royal Army Veterinary Corps

The Royal Army Veterinary Corps of today is small, but carries out a most important function in the modern army. There are still horses to be bought, trained and cared for, while mules are used for pack transport in mountainous terrain.

All corps training is done at the RAVC Training Centre and Depot, Melton Mowbray. This includes riding, stable and kennel management, and nursing and treatment of sick animals. Providing they show the right potential during training, recruits have the opportunity of being trained as farriers, saddlers and riding instructors.

Being small and mainly specialist, the RAVC carries a very high percentage of non-commissioned officers—many of whom are expected to work independently in charge of detachments—giving good prospects of advancement to warrant officer and for commissioned rank in a quartermaster category.

School leavers can join the Household Cavalry or the Royal Army Veterinary Corps at any Army Careers Information Office, whose location can be obtained from a local post office.

CHAPTER FOUR

Training in Agriculture

A job in agriculture can offer one of the most satisfying careers open to young people—where they will be in daily contact with real life, not just the television version of it. The field covers everything from dairy farming to growing wheat, hill sheep farming to potato cultivation, and cattle farming to intensive crop production. Anyone interested in working with farm animals will find ample openings and good prospects with dairy cattle, beef cattle and pig farming. All candidates for such a career should follow the advice given here by the Agricultural Training Board:

A job in agriculture demands workers who are able to adapt themselves to new conditions and to understand the complex processes involved in the growth of plants and animals. Most farm workers today are required to drive a tractor and operate a variety of specialised machines of one sort or another. For just as the grain harvest has now been completely mechanised, good progress is being made towards the mechanised harvesting of other crops, such as sugar beet and potatoes, and the feeding of livestock.

Over half a million people—farmers and farm workers—are occupied full-time in agriculture. Some of the occupations in the industry are available to women as well as to men. Opportunities for new entrants are more interesting than ever before. Wage rates may be lower than in comparable industrial jobs, but skill, responsibility and experience are rewarded. Those with appropriate technical training and supervisory ability can certainly look forward to good conditions and salaries.

TECHNICAL TRAINING

Anyone seeking a successful career in such an up-to-date industry should have technical training. Young men and women can no longer be expected to pick up farming skills as they go along. The New Entrant (Apprentice) Training Scheme provides an attractive opening, by which entrants may be indentured to a training farmer for a period of three years. They attend further education classes during that period and take proficiency tests. There is also a whole range of full-time and part-time courses at agricultural colleges and institutes.

The New Entrant Training Scheme

Systematic training of new entrants brings benefits to all. Employers benefit because workers quickly reach competent standards of work, avoiding much of the wastage and damage to animals, crops and machines often associated with inexperienced workers. As trainees reach maturity, employers benefit from improved quality and increased quantity of output, and from reductions in working costs.

Employees obtain greater satisfaction from work which they can do well, and this leads to the development of a responsible attitude to their work. Most workers in the industry work for long periods without close supervision; they operate expensive equipment and are concerned with living things, so this sense of responsibility for the employer's resources is of vital importance.

Special emphasis during the impressionable years of training is given to safe practices and attention to the wellbeing of stock and crops. Sound training in today's technology is vital to ensure that those involved have a firm foundation on which to keep up with future advances.

The New Entrant Training Scheme draws upon the invaluable experience of farmers and growers to join in the training of new entrants to the industry, thus minimising the cost of training.

Local supervision

Farmers, growers and workers serve on the Agricultural Training Board's area training committees and the Scottish training committee to ensure that the training given meets local requirements. In many cases, sub-committees have been set up to deal with the detailed administration of the scheme. They have four main tasks:

1 to consider applications from employers who wish to register their holdings as suitable for training under the scheme;
2 to consider applications from young people and others who wish to train under the scheme;
3 to supervise the training of each trainee, through progress reports from the Board's area training advisers;
4 to deal with social and welfare matters affecting the training and to settle any problems which may arise during training.

Categories of training

The industry's production comes from five main sectors: general agriculture, crop production, livestock production, poultry production and horticulture. Each of these sectors is further divided into training categories—livestock being divided into milk production, beef production, sheep production and pig production.

Training may be undertaken in any category and consists of practical training on the holding, attendance by day or block release at a centre of further education, and passing specified proficiency tests. Details are given in *Craft Training Requirements* booklets published by the Agricultural Training Board.

Trainees can choose their category on joining the scheme or delay their choice until the beginning of the second year. Those who still find it difficult to decide can follow programmes under the general categories which will give them a good broad training in the main skills of the industry.

Certain skills are basic to most of the agricultural categories and all trainees are expected to qualify in these jobs, including tractor driving and maintenance. All livestock and poultry trainees have to train for the essential tasks involving the control, feeding, health assessment, cleaning and bedding of stock, as well as acquiring skills in the various routine tasks associated with the operation and maintenance of selected mechanical farm equipment.

Selection and entry of trainees

Trainees of all ages are accepted for training under the scheme, but it is expected that young people will form the majority of new entrants. Older men or women who have spent some time in the industry may also apply for training under the scheme; their existing standard of competence in the category of training required will be assessed as a preliminary to acceptance.

Candidates should have a real interest in agriculture or horticulture, with good practical ability and application. This is important, for during training instruction is given in many practical skills, and ability is assessed by taking proficiency tests.

Applications for training should be sent to the local area or regional office of the Board. Ideally training should commence in the autumn to coincide with the beginning of the academic year. Applications made at other times of the year are considered, but some delay may arise in arranging the trainee's further education.

All applications are considered by the local committee responsible for the selection of trainees. In some cases candidates are called for interview, when the parents or guardians of applicants under the age of eighteen are also invited to attend. Sons or daughters of farmers may apply to become trainees under the scheme and the question of whether or not they should be trained on their parents' holdings is decided at the time of entry.

Arrangements are made for placing a trainee with a training employer in a suitable area after a candidate has been accepted for training. For those under eighteen, this is normally arranged by the local careers officer of the Youth Employment Service, who may be assisted by the Board's Area Training Adviser.

THE FUTURE FOR SKILLED PERSONNEL

The *Careers in Agriculture* leaflet published by the Agricultural Training Board outlines the following categories:

Skilled workers

Farms in Britain are increasing in size and there is a pronounced trend towards specialisation. The total number of farm workers is likely to continue to decrease, but in the smaller labour force of the future there will be an urgent need for better-trained and highly skilled personnel.

Relatively few people now working in the industry are general farm workers and the new entrant should aim to become a skilled stockman, shepherd, pigman or cowman, a machinery operator or farm mechanic.

From the status of skilled worker, promotion to foreman or farm manager is possible.

Foremen

There are many opportunities for young men to take charge of dairy and pig herds or poultry flocks, and to take on the responsibility of supervising other skilled men. These jobs attract premium rates and often include production bonuses.

Farm managers

The farm manager is expected to look after the day-to-day running of the farm, the control of the staff, the organisation of field and other work, the marketing of farm produce and the maintenance of business records. In fact, he supervises and carries out the policy that has been laid down for the farm. He holds an interesting and responsible post with an income reflecting the high qualities demanded.

Farmers

In order to run a profitable enterprise on his own account, the modern farmer must be skilled and energetic. But the main problem for those who wish to begin farming is capital. For some years now, with land prices steadily rising, it has been increasingly difficult to find farms to rent and, although many of today's most successful farmers began with a rented smallholding, the chances of a beginner in the industry becoming a tenant farmer these days are slim.

In addition to adequate finance, it is emphasised that a thorough training in agricultural science and farm business management is vital to all aspiring farmers. A sound general education, with a bias towards science, up to the age of eighteen, followed by some years of practical experience and a two- or three-year course at an agricultural college, or pursuing the New Entrant Training Scheme, should be every candidate's objective.

FURTHER INFORMATION

Young people interested in a career in agriculture, with special reference to livestock farming, can obtain helpful advice from careers officers of the Youth Employment Service, careers teachers and the county agricultural college. Addresses and telephone numbers of the county secretary of the National Farmers' Union of England and Wales and the area secretary of the National Farmers' Union of Scotland are available from the telephone directory. Other useful addresses include:

The Agricultural Training Board, Bourne House, 32/34 Beckenham Road, Beckenham, Kent BR3 4PB.

The Agricultural Education Association, Staffordshire College of Agriculture, Rodbaston, Penkridge, Stafford.

Royal Agricultural Society of England, 35 Belgrave Square, London SW1.

Royal Highland and Agricultural Society of Scotland, 8 Eglinton Crescent, Edinburgh 12.

Royal Welsh Agricultural Society, Llanelwedd, Buith Wells, Breconshire.

Women's Farm and Garden Association, Courtauld House, Byng Place, London WC1.

Catalogues of publications dealing with sources of information about general agriculture, livestock and meat, dairying, pig husbandry, and poultry and eggs are obtainable free from The Library, Ministry of Agriculture, Fisheries and Food, Whitehall Place, London SW1 3HH (Tel 01-839 7711 Ext 7192). A few publications are available from colleges and public libraries, either from stock or through regional or national lending schemes.

A DAY'S WORK ON A DAIRY FARM

Every student of dairy farming may at some time or another undertake a typical day's work similar to the ones I experienced on a large dairy farm near Maiden Newton, in Dorset. It was my intention at the time to undergo a diploma course at an agricultural college, and I had joined the farm's labour force for the required year of practical farm-work prior to admission. My term of work began in the winter month of October and during the initial stages I struggled to get to know a herd of some seventy-six pedigree short-horned dairy cattle.

04.40 Getting up at what some consider to be an unsociable hour, to my surprise, presented few hardships, probably due to the fact that my enthusiasm for working with animals overrode any natural inclination not to rise before daybreak. A two-mile bicycle ride from my lodgings to the cowsheds dispersed any vestige of cobwebbing from the previous evening.

05.00 At the dairy I donned heavy seaman-type oil-skins and

wellingtons, so that in spite of steady rain I could venture forth into a 12-acre meadow in search of the seventy-six cows that had to be rounded up and herded in the direction of the spacious farm yard.

05.20 Stumbling, slipping and falling over the hilly, drenched terrain, before the first light of a winter morning, was a good initiation into the life of a dairyman and the ways of dairy cattle. The first objective was the bulky form of Thelma, for once she had been located and mobilised the rest of the herd would be well on their way down the muddy track towards the dairy. Thelma always moved in her own time and nothing on earth could persuade her to do otherwise; she would just plod towards her morning feed, her muddy tail swinging nonchalantly as her rear-guard.

06.00 By the time I had managed to close the four-barred farmyard gate behind the herd, the dairyman and his wife had the cowshed in full operation, with twenty of the cows already in the stalls. The cowshed was equipped with modern machinery—a ten-unit Alfa Laval combine milker. Each cow had a chain fixed loosely around its neck to prevent it from moving about too much and to minimise any damage to the milking cups. There were two cows to each stall; whilst one was being milked, the other could be cleaned down and made ready for milking. The machine took the milk directly from the udder into a graded bottle suspended some 2½ft above the cow's back. This gave the dairyman the opportunity to record the milk yield and, if necessary, the butter fat content from each cow. The milk then flowed from the bottle along the piping to the cooling machine in the dairy.

08.30 By this time the whole herd was milked, and each cow had been given a feed concentrate in the form of cubes, as well as a quantity of hay and as much water as required. The lorry from the local milk marketing board would have collected the milk churns from the dairy; these full ten-gallon churns were loaded on to the lorry from a ramp at the same level, a task which always taxed my muscles to straining point. Whilst the cows were still in the yard, I would spend an extremely active period sweeping and hosing down the entire cowshed area, and then help the dairyman and his wife to finish off the cleaning, washing and sterilising of the milking-machine equipment.

09.30 Most mornings I drove the herd to a nearby kale field of strip grazing, where I would move the electric fence forward a further 10yd to provide the short-horned cattle with the extra feed to aid their milk yield.

09.30 – 12.00 The remainder of the morning was taken up by helping with the sterilising of any milking equipment, including the piping, bottles and cooling system, that had not been done previously. Hay and cow nuts had to be replenished in each stall, and then the vast area of cement covering the spacious yard next to the sheds was swept and hosed down.

14.00 Work was much slacker in the earlier part of the afternoon. Sometimes, under the direction of the head dairyman, matings would be arranged, with a visit by a representative from the Ministry of Agriculture, who would administer the artificial insemination and make the necessary recording in the herd's pedigree book.

14.45 The herd was brought in from the kale field and the milking procedure would be repeated.

16.15 As soon as the last cow had been released from its stall, I would guide the herd to the 12-acre meadow where the cows spent the night. The dairyman and his wife meanwhile saw to the cleaning and sterilising of the milking equipment.

I found the work as a trainee dairyman harder physically than mentally, although recognising that the production of milk is a highly skilled profession.

The discomforts of winter work on a farm in England can be blamed chiefly on the climate. Frequent drenchings when moving electric fences amongst saturated kale and walking with the cattle; the feeling of cold, with numb hands, whilst hosing down large areas of disinterested cement were well compensated for by the many joys that work with farm animals can bring—such as watching cows calving and the subsequent rearing of heifers. Apart from the welfare of the animals, the study of nutrition and the challenging prospect of increasing the average milk yield for each cow make this a worthwhile and satisfying job.

CHAPTER FIVE

Poultry Farming

Over the past twenty-five years, the expansion of the poultry industry in the British Isles has been astronomical. Today, it offers a wide variety of opportunity, whether in a large company or as a self-employed farmer or as a general poultryman. Technical training is obtainable at universities and agricultural colleges; degrees and diplomas being awarded on the completion of three-year courses. Naturally graduates will be seeking managerial appointments at the start of their career, but much of the man power in the industry today is made up of non-qualified people.

A large poultry farm is usually left in the hands of a farm manager with full- and/or part-time assistants. The manager will be salaried and expected to work hours as required for the efficient running of the unit. His assistants will be paid a weekly wage for a 40-hour week—the normal agricultural working week—and any extra hours required at weekends will be paid at the overtime rate: time and a half on Saturdays and week-day evenings, and double time on Sundays. These wage rates vary considerably from farm to farm, depending, for example, on whether the worker has a rent-free cottage, and in most cases the remuneration would be in excess of the minimum NFU rates.

Farm workers are not highly paid compared with other industries, but the life has many compensations. The responsibility of controlling a unit containing stock worth many thousands of pounds is a goal which many young men would be grateful to have in sight. A young man (or woman), after gaining practical experience for a few years, may find himself in sole charge of a very large business enterprise. There are not many industries today where advancement can be so rapid.

The Agricultural Training Board publishes some excellent literature on careers in the poultry industry, from which I quote:

The poultry industry's development is the result of harnessing technological advances to a long established agricultural pursuit. Until the 1940s the business of poultry farming was only a side-line on most farms and often the responsibility of the farmers' womenfolk. Today, whilst many general farms still have their poultry flocks, most poultry farming enterprises have become large and highly specialised businesses.

The leading breeders now operate with thousands of breeding birds; the larger hatcheries distribute chicks by the 100,000 each week; there are many chicken rearers with an annual output of a million birds, and some egg producers supply eggs by the million. The establishment of very large poultry units, either on the specialised or general farm, has stimulated a rapidly rising demand for properly trained men and women to work in them.

The poultry industry requires people with a wide range of qualifications or skills, ranging from scientists to trained technicians and highly skilled workers. Many of the latter enter the industry as trainees and obtain the necessary abilities through various further education and training schemes, such as the New Entrant (Apprentice) Training Scheme. Young men and women entering the poultry industry through this scheme are indentured to a training employer for a period of three years. They attend further education classes during that period and take proficiency tests.

The specialist breeding undertakings now employ people with a high level of scientific training, particularly geneticists and statisticians, and some firms are large enough to need electronic computers. Experts in nutrition and other applied sciences are also required by many organisations, particularly the advisory services and food compounding companies.

Whatever the size of the flock, the skills of sound animal husbandry are of basic importance to scientific poultry farming.

OPPORTUNITIES AND PROSPECTS

The complexity of this branch of agriculture has led to a great variety of job opportunities for people working directly or in association with poultry. As well as many routine occupations, the work ranges from that of the stockman, with his day-to-day management of a flock of moderate size, to the manager of a much larger unit employing several stockmen, and to administrative positions requiring specialised training at graduate or postgraduate level and/or a high standard of experience in general poultry husbandry.

Occupations are in many cases equally suitable for men and women. The working poultryman or poultrywoman will normally receive the agricultural wage, with additions in recognition of specialised skills. The managerial posts, which vary according to the size of the unit and degree of responsibility, carry attractive salaries and often a free house. In some of the larger organisations, well-qualified managers earn considerably more. Managerial posts are usually on the farm and the manager is in daily contact with the stock being supervised.

QUALITIES AND QUALIFICATIONS

Stockmen

A prospective poultryman or woman should like the idea of working with poultry; be prepared to work variable hours, possibly alone; prefer working in the country; be prepared to live away from home and to move periodically to gain experience; be able to work to a plan and yet be observant. Education standards are not so important, provided the poultryman is capable of maintaining the day-to-day records needed on the unit.

A poultryman should acquire as much practical training in stockmanship as possible and also seek to gain instruction in the application of more theoretical knowledge. Details of particular training are given in the job leaflets obtainable from the Agricultural Training Board. For the senior poultryman looking towards farm managerial posts, a formal qualification following a residential course at a teaching institution is a normal requirement.

Unit managers

A farm or unit manager, having all the qualities of an efficient poultryman, should be proficient in the basic principles of staff management and work organisation, and be receptive to new techniques and capable of evaluating them. A good secondary education is desirable, with particular attention to chemistry and/or biology.

Senior posts

An adviser must be a good mixer, willing to spend a fair time in travel, able to demonstrate or lecture, and to 'translate' scientific principles into everyday practice. His is mainly outdoor work. An aptitude for teaching, in addition to the qualities for lecturing, are needed for this position, as well as the ability to keep abreast of technical development.

For the institutional courses leading to a qualification needed for an adviser's post, a pass at GCE 'O' level, or equivalent, in four subjects (including English language and approved science subjects) is almost certain to be required.

For appointments necessitating specialist knowledge of genetics, nutrition, statistics or other science subjects, a degree in the appropriate subjects, and preferably postgraduate work connected with poultry, is customarily expected.

FURTHER INFORMATION

Young people interested in a career in poultry husbandry can seek advice from careers officers of the Youth Employment Service and from careers teachers.

Information on education, training and career prospects may be obtained from the county secretary of the National Farmers' Union of England and Wales, or the area secretary of the National Farmers' Union of Scotland, whose addresses and telephone numbers may be found in the telephone directory.

Leaflets in the *Careers in Poultry Husbandry* series—*Working with Poultry*; *Egg Production*; *Meat Production*—are obtainable from the Agricultural Training Board, Bourne House, 32/34 Beckenham Road, Kent BR3 4PB.

Information is also obtainable from: British Federation of Poultry Industries, High Holborn House, 52/54 High Holborn, London WC1, and the National Poultry Diploma Board Ltd, Golden Buffs, Burney Bit, Pamber Heath, Basingstoke, Hampshire.

BROILER BREEDING

Mr Noel Surridge, who runs a highly successful broiler breeding farm, at Horam, Sussex, gives his first-hand assessment of this branch of the poultry industry:

The broiler industry has been a part of British farming life for almost twenty years, although technical advancement has been most marked during the last five years. Today, not only is the broiler industry a particularly specialised part of poultry farming, but within the industry itself each stage in the cycle has become specialised.

The main stages in the production of broiler chicken are:

1 Management of the parent breeding stock
2 Incubation of hatching eggs provided by above
3 Growing of the resultant day-old broiler chicks
4 Processing to provide the finished product

Intensive poultry keeping is normally carried out in custom-built houses equipped with all the necessary amenities, such as electric light, main water and a controlled ventilation system. Houses can vary in size, but the maximum is probably not more than 15,000sq ft. This area should be sub-divided into sections of approximately 1,000–1,500sq ft so that the flock may be divided into pens of not more than 500 birds.

It is normal practice for the flock to be reared on the same site from day-old. The birds do not come into lay until 24 weeks of age; thus the daily routine follows one pattern during the rearing period (0–24 weeks) and one during the laying period (25–62 weeks).

The rearing period

The house and equipment must be ready several days before the day-old chicks arrive and the brooders (usually Calor gas fired) are lit 48 hours beforehand. Initial brooding temperature should be not less than 95° F, although the behaviour of the chicks is the best guide to optimum temperature. If they are too hot, they will keep as far away from the direct heat as possible; conversely, they will huddle directly under the heaters if the ambient temperature is too low. Males and females are reared separately until they are ready to be mated at 20 weeks.

For the first 5 weeks of their life the chicks are fed 'ad lib', when they are allowed to consume as much as they are able. The starter ration is supplied in the form of crumbs, but after a week or ten days mash can be substituted. Care must be taken not to waste the feed by over-filling the troughs as spillage is almost immediately lost in the litter. Continuous clean drinking water must be available at all times and the mechanism of the drinkers must be checked frequently, as a leaking drinker can flood the surrounding area in a very short time.

As the birds get older the feed intake is increased but has to be carefully controlled. Broiler breeders have a tendency to put on weight rapidly to the detriment of egg production later on, and it has become the accepted practice to limit their nutrient intake from about 6 weeks of age onwards. In order to administer this practice, an accurate count of the birds must be available at all times and accurate mortality records must always be kept.

The most reliable guide to the effectiveness of a chosen feeding programme is a careful check on live-weight of the birds—a sample 10 per cent of the flock is weighed weekly, and the amount of feed increased or decreased accordingly.

Vaccination is another important routine which is carried out periodically. This is designed to prevent outbreaks of infectious bronchitis, Newcastle disease (fowl pest) and Mareks disease. Where live vaccine is used, this is administered to the whole flock in the drinking water; in the case of dead vaccine, each bird has to be individually caught and injected.

During the rearing period the daily tasks can be summarised as follows:

Feeding twice a day (morning and afternoon); quantities of feed are weighed daily.

Constant check on behavioural pattern of the birds to determine the condition of the growing birds. Any weak or injured birds are isolated or given remedial treatment.

Routine maintenance of equipment. Nest boxes must be in position and littered with wood shavings by the time the birds are 22 weeks of age.

The laying period

Once the birds come into lay, production rises very rapidly from 0–80 per cent or more in 7 or 8 weeks. By the time peak production is reached, all routines must have been standardised, in particular the times of feeding and egg collections, as the birds are very susceptible to change.

FEEDING There are three recognised methods of feeding a flock of broiler breeders:

1 Automatically. Mash from a bulk feed hopper is carried in a trough by chain link down one side of the flock house and back down the other. A time clock operates the mechanism twice a day.
2 In feeders. Galvanised tube feeders suspended off the floor (8 for every 100 birds) are filled manually in the morning with the required amount for the day.
3 Floor feeding. Pellets are scattered on the litter three times a day, usually to coincide with egg collection times.

An additional feed of grain (barley or oats) is given last thing at night.

EGG COLLECTION Eggs should be collected at least three times a day. They are collected in wire baskets and counted at the time of collection to ensure that production records of each pen are available. By this stage in the birds' life, feed intake is geared not to body weight but to egg production, and variations are made accordingly.

Once the eggs have been collected, they are then fumigated (preferably while still warm) in a cabinet. The fumigant is produced by mixing crystals of potassium permanganate with liquid formalin. The reaction of these two chemicals produces formaldehyde gas. This process lasts for approximately 20–30 minutes, after which time the eggs are ready for grading, cleaning, packing and storing.

GRADING Egg size, shape and shell quality are the controlling items for this operation. Most commercial hatcheries will only accept eggs for hatching over $1\frac{11}{16}$ oz in weight. Inferior shell quality will result in eggs being broken in the incubators and these eggs should therefore not be used for hatching.

CLEANING Eggs should never be washed but cleaned with sand paper to ensure that contamination from the shell of one egg cannot be transferred to another. Bacterial infection which is easily absorbed in water has the most detrimental effect on hatchability.

PACKING AND STORING A small room must be available for storage of hatching eggs until they are ready to be collected. If possible, this should be controlled at a temperature of 55–60° F with a relative humidity of 80–85 per cent.

The daily tasks during the laying period might be as follows:

07.00 First feed. Adjust ventilation throughout the flock house. Pick up any floor eggs. Remove carcasses of birds which have died during previous 24 hours, and record these pen by pen. Check condition of birds in isolation coops and fill water troughs.

09.00 Second feed, and first egg collection.

12.00 Third feed, and second egg collection.

15.30 Fourth feed, and third egg collection.

Egg packing takes place in between these times as circumstances permit.

GAME BIRD FARMS

As agriculture becomes more intensive, the economic usage of marginal land is essential and an increasing number of farms are leasing such land to shooting syndicates for stocking with game birds.

Game farms like the Northern Pheasantries, Tatham, Lancaster, and the Moor End Game Farm, Whitby, North Yorkshire, are members of the Game Farmers Association, the Game Conservancy, and the British Field Sports Society. These farms offer a wide selection of domestic pheasant breeds: blackneck, ringneck, melanistic, Chinese and Mongolian, which they sell at the following stages: eggs (per 100), day-olds (per 100), 6-week-olds, 8-week-olds, adult pheasants from laying pens, and fully-winged pheasants available for shoots in early spring.

The Craven Game Farms—under the personal supervision of

Mr Alan Robinson, a countryman with a tremendous knowledge of the outdoor—concentrate on breeding a hardy stock of game birds at Kelbrook, Yorkshire. Pheasant eggs; pheasant poults; Japanese quail—eggs and adult birds; mallard—eggs, day-olds, six-week-olds, are all offered for sale by the hundred. The adoption of modern breeding methods, using the latest incubators, and breeding from strong, hardy stock, have rapidly increased the farms' reputation throughout the game-rearing world. Many thousand quail alone are sold weekly to shoots and restaurants.

Anyone intrigued with the bird species bred and reared on game farms, and wishing to specialise in this field, is well advised to take advantage of the New Entrant (Apprentice) Training Scheme. The Game Conservancy at Fordingbridge, Hampshire, which runs courses on the breeding and rearing of game birds, in particular pheasants, grouse, partridge and mallard, may provide helpful guidance at a later stage, as well as advising on the most profitable use of marginal land for game birds.

CHAPTER SIX

The Veterinary Profession

I recall certain members of the pony fraternity at my first school telling me they were going to become veterinary surgeons, as this would be the only job open to people who wanted to work with animals. What some of them had not bargained for was that they would have to do a lot of hard work before even qualifying for entrance to a university providing courses leading to vetinary science degrees.

The popular image of a veterinary surgeon—prodding cows with a shooting stick and talking wisely to the farmer about the herd's chances of pulling off some prizes at the county agricultural show—is far from typical. For, as the booklet *A Career as a Veterinary Surgeon*, published by The Royal College of Veterinary Surgeons, states:

> It is not always realised just how important a part the veterinarian plays in the health and productive capacity of farm stock and how great have been the advances in veterinary medicine and surgery appertaining to both farm and domestic animals in recent years, and that increasing numbers of veterinary graduates are required for research and teaching posts in the universities, research institutes, government services and in industry. Every branch of the veterinary profession has

important contributions to make now and in the future.

The following information about a career in veterinary medicine has been made available by the Royal College of Veterinary Surgeons:

ENTRANCE TO A UNIVERSITY

Six universities in the United Kingdom—Bristol, Cambridge, Edinburgh, Glasgow, Liverpool and London—and two in Eire—the National University of Ireland and the University of Dublin—provide courses of instruction leading to a veterinary degree. The course normally lasts between five and six years.

Candidates must fulfil minimum registration requirements of the university of their choice and any other course requirements specified. Applications should be made to the registrars of the universities for particulars of entry requirements and to the deans of the veterinary schools for course requirements. Students admitted to veterinary schools normally hold good advanced or higher level passes in chemistry, physics and biology, but those with good advanced or higher level passes in other related subjects are also considered. Those still at school and contemplating a veterinary career should discuss this with head teachers or careers teachers.

Applications for entry to Bristol, Cambridge, Edinburgh, Glasgow, Liverpool and London universities' veterinary schools must be made through the Universities Central Council on Admissions (UCCA), except as indicated below; information can be obtained from the secretary. Applications for entry are made approximately one year in advance, the precise dates being obtained from the UCCA. Applicants for entry to Cambridge must also submit a preliminary application form direct to the college of their choice, within the university. Applicants in the United Kingdom who wish to apply only to Glasgow should do so direct to the university and not through the UCCA. Inquiries regarding admission to the National University of Ireland (University College) and to the University of Dublin (Trinity College) should be addressed to the authorities of the university concerned. (For addresses see pages 82–3).

A great deal of useful information is given in the booklet *How to Apply for Admission to a University*, published annually by UCCA. It includes a definition of an overseas candidate and of a United Kingdom candidate, giving full details on the method of applying for entrance. Copies of the booklet are sent to schools in June, together with application forms for entry to universities in October of the following year. The latest date for receipt by the UCCA offices of applications for admission to universities including Cambridge is 15 October and not including Cambridge 15 December.

Overseas candidates may be accepted for first degree courses under conditions laid down by the universities. The fees charged to overseas students are higher than those for other students and details may be obtained from the universities. There are advantages in training undergraduates in their own country or in a country with similar livestock and husbandry practices. This should be borne in mind before application is made.

The number of applications for entry to veterinary schools exceeds the number of places available, and applicants who satisfy entry and course requirements are not necessarily guaranteed a place.

VETERINARY DEGREE COURSES

A veterinary student is required to pass the appropriate university examinations and will eventually obtain the veterinary degree of his university. The actual name and style of the degree is the prerogative of the university, but all these veterinary degrees confer upon the holders the right to membership of the Royal College of Veterinary Surgeons, the governing body of the profession. Under the provisions of the Veterinary Surgeons Act, 1966, with certain minor exceptions, no person is permitted to undertake diagnosis and treatment of the ailments of animals unless he or she is a registered veterinarian, ie unqualified practice is not permitted by law.

Taking one of the six universities in the United Kingdom providing veterinary courses, the University of Bristol veterinary degree course extends over five years and leads to the degree of Bachelor of Veterinary Science (BVSc). There are usually 150 veterinary undergraduates at any one time, some 30 students being admitted annually, about eight of whom are girls.

The first three years (the pre-clinical years) provide the necessary grounding in the basic veterinary sciences. The first year seeks to combine the practical approach of a full course in animal management, with weekly visits to the Langford Veterinary School, about 14 miles from Bristol, for practice in animal handling, with the more theoretical subjects of biochemistry and physiology. In the third year, these lead on to the study of disease processes, covered in courses in the subjects of pathology, microbiology, parasitology. There are also further studies during this year of the animal husbandry group of subjects, with agrostology, animal behaviour, housing and genetics. There is full integration in these first three years with medical and science departments, so that the veterinary student has daily contact with those studying for medical, dental and science degrees. He will, during these years, be centred in Bristol, working partly in the Veterinary School, partly in the Medical School. For those achieving a high enough placing in the class lists, the opportunity is open to intercalate a year reading for an honours BSc degree in one of the subjects they have been studying.

The fourth and fifth (final years) are the clinical years, with the students in residence at the Langford Veterinary School. Students spend much time in the Departments of Veterinary Medicine and Veterinary Surgery, but there are also the husbandry subjects of nutrition and reproduction, along with special pathology, parasitology and meat hygiene. With clinical clerking, clinico-pathological conferences and project work, much of the teaching is in small groups and of a less formal character. Further information may be obtained from the Registrar, University of Bristol, Senate House, Bristol BS8 1TH.

POSTGRADUATE TRAINING

The veterinary profession, though numerically small, has important duties to perform. In general practice it is responsible for the maintenance of health and production of farm animals, for the prevention of disease and for the medical and surgical treatment of all animals including household pets and zoo animals. Veterinary research and teaching in the schools is constantly expanding. The Ministry of Agriculture, Fisheries and Food maintains a large field staff for the control of the major epidemic diseases. Research is undertaken in the Ministry's laboratories, the veterinary schools, and research institutes and departments financed by the government or by private enterprise. There are also opportunities for service in commerce and industry, in the public health field and in countries overseas. Students who wish to make a career in biological research will find ample opportunity in the profession.

Training facilities for postgraduates at universities with veterinary schools vary from one university to another. At the University of Bristol a graduate wishing to obtain an honours BSc degree in one of the pre-clinical science subjects (anatomy, pharmacology, physiology, biochemistry, microbiology) may be accepted by the department concerned. The year of study that is necessary is generally an intercalated one.

The degree of MSc within the faculty of science by research is open to veterinary graduates and may be completed in either one or two calendar years. The PhD degree within the faculty of medicine is most commonly obtained by veterinarians after two years of whole-time research, although more usually three years are taken to complete the degree. Sometimes a candidate's supervisor for both MSc or PhD will specify certain course work that must be undertaken.

Training for the RCVS's more recently established Diplomas

in Veterinary Radiology and Veterinary Anaesthesia (the DVR and DVA) can be undertaken in the Department of Veterinary Surgery at the Langford School.

AWARDS FOR UNDERGRADUATE AND GRADUATE STUDIES

The local education authorities of England and Wales are empowered to make awards to all suitably qualified students accepted for first degrees and comparable courses of study at universities in the United Kingdom. The value of the awards (subject to the maximum value at any given time) depends on the income of the parents and of the student. Similar arrangements operate in Northern Ireland.

In Scotland the students' allowances, administered centrally by the Scottish Education Department, correspond to the awards made by the local education authorities in England and Wales.

As details of the awards available to the postgraduate, and the amounts payable under each kind of award, are constantly changing, this information is published in a leaflet separate to the RCVS booklet, *A Career as a Veterinary Surgeon*. In May 1973, the main awards offered by professional, governmental, scientific and educational organisations for studies undertaken in the United Kingdom and Ireland ranged from the RCVS Trust Fund's 'The International League for Protection of Horses Scholarship' (which has a trust fund of £1,000 per annum for a maximum period of three years, with up to £200 per annum for expenses, and is tenable at any university in the United Kingdom) to an award of up to £3,500 per annum grant, depending on age and experience, of the Animal Health Trusts' Wooldridge Livestock Research Fellowship (which allows reasonable expenses to be made available to veterinary graduates for work of direct importance to livestock production).

FURTHER INFORMATION

Youth Employment Officers will be glad to give any help they can to young people interested in a veterinary career. The following publications provide comprehensive information:

The booklet *A Career as a Veterinary Surgeon*: from the Registrar, Royal College of Veterinary Surgeons, 32 Belgrave Square, London SW1X 8QP.

The Veterinary Science Degree Course Guide: from the Careers Research and Advisory Centre, Bateman Street, Cambridge.

The booklet *How to Apply for Admission to a University*: from the Universities Central Council on Admissions (UCCA), PO Box 28, Cheltenham, Gloucestershire GL50 1HY.

The veterinary degree course is listed under UCCA code number 2400 and the UCCA code number for each university is given under separate headings. From information provided by the Royal College of Veterinary Surgeons, the following table has been compiled for easy guidance and reference:

University	*Total of veterinary students (approx)*	*Number admitted annually (approx)*	*Duration of course*	*Degree*
The Bursar, University of Bristol (UCCA Code No 12) Senate House, Bristol BS8 1TH	150	30	5 years	BVSc
The Administrative Secretary, University of Cambridge (UCCA Code No 15) School of Veterinary Medicine, Madingley Road, Cambridge	—	25	3 years 6 years	BA VetMB
The Dean, University of Edinburgh (UCCA Code No 22) Faculty of Veterinary Medicine, Royal (Dick) School of Veterinary Studies, Summerhall, Edinburgh EH9 1QH	270	55	5 years	BVM&S

University	*Total of veterinary students (approx)*	*Number admitted annually (approx)*	*Duration of course*	*Degree*
The Registrar (UCCA Code No 25) University of Glasgow, Glasgow W2	250	50–5	5 years	BVMS
The Dean, University of Liverpool (UCCA Code No 35) Faculty of Veterinary Science, The University, PO Box 147, Liverpool L69 3BX	180–200	40	5 years	BVSc
The Registrar (UCCA Code No 48) The Royal Veterinary College, Royal College Street, London NW1 0TU	300	65	4 years 2 terms	BVetMed
School of Veterinary Medicine, University of Dublin, Trinity College, Ballsbridge, Dublin 4	60	15	5 years	MVB
The National University of Ireland, University College, Dublin	—	55	5 years	MVB

CAREER OPPORTUNITIES

The RCVS revised leaflet (May 1973) states that about 70 per cent of all veterinary surgeons working in Britain are in private practice. Students will have had the opportunity during their veterinary degree course to observe conditions and openings in this branch of the profession. Salaries in general practice for newly qualified assistants are usually higher than in first appointments to other branches of the profession and are normally in excess of £2,000. An assistant, after some years of acquiring experience in veterinary practice, may hope to purchase a practice or acquire a partnership in one.

Many veterinary practices deal with both farm animals (which may include poultry) and domestic pets, the proportion of time devoted to each category depending to a considerable extent on the location of the practice. Others, particularly in the larger urban areas, devote their time exclusively to small animal work, sometimes including cage birds and such exotic pets as monkeys, lizards and tropical fish. In a good number of practices, veterinarians spend part of their time dealing with pleasure ponies and horses, and bloodstock. A few practices deal exclusively with equine work or farm animals or poultry. Veterinarians in general practice, especially in the agricultural areas, are also called upon to advise in the preventive medicine field.

A VETERINARY SURGEON'S WORKING DAY

The majority of the veterinary practices in the British Isles are no longer operated by one man or woman, but consist of several veterinarians working in partnership, with or without more junior members of the profession acting as assistants to the principals or partners.

Mr David Jemson, BA, VetMB, MRCVS, belongs to a four-man practice in Devizes, Wiltshire, in which all are equal partners. The practice handles approximately 70 per cent large animal work (farm animals) and about 30 per cent small animals (dogs and cats). He describes a typical working day, starting at 09.00 hours when a surgery for small animals is held:

'The first case that came into surgery was a lady with a cat whose front paw was badly swollen. The paw was very painful; the cat had a high temperature and would not eat. This cat was suffering from an infected foot almost certainly due to a bite from another cat. An injection of penicillin and streptomycin was given, which rarely fails to cure the condition quickly.

'A dog was then brought in with a 3in gash on its flank. This dog was put into the hospital to have the wound sutured under general anaesthetic.

'An eight-week-old labrador pup came next, to have the first of two injections to immunise it against hard pad and distemper.

'An old dog came in, the owner said that the dog, which was eleven years old, had a cough and seemed to puff and pant very quickly when exercised. Examination showed a heart failing to maintain the circulation due to leaky valves and congested lungs. Diuretic and heart stimulant were given, and an appointment made to see the dog in four days' time.

'Next came a dog with an exceedingly irritable skin. The dog was found to have fleas causing an eczema. Dusting powder was given to kill the fleas and some antihistamine tablets to check the inflammatory reaction in the skin.

'By 10.30 no further animals were presented at the surgery. A quick cup of coffee is made by our receptionist-secretary, who is the hub of communications within the practice, taking all the in-coming telephone calls during the day and relaying them to the partners on the rounds if necessary. It is time for me to go out on my rounds.

'My first call was to a farm about five miles away. The farmer had a lame cow. The cow was in the milking parlour, and was lame in one hind foot. The cow's leg was lifted up by putting on a rope round the hock and running the rope round a bar above. The sole of the foot showed a little black mark on it which was pared out with a knife, eventually releasing some pus from a small abscess. The hole this made was filled with a paste which would draw out any more pus and the cow was given an injection.

'After completing this rather dirty and strenuous job I moved on to another farm nearby where a cow which had calved five days before had not yet discharged the placenta. She would not eat her food and was running a temperature. I put on an arm-length disposable plastic glove and put my arm into the cow's vagina and womb to detach the placenta. This was removed in about five minutes and two aureomycin pessaries put in the womb to kill the infection. An antibiotic injection was given (twenty-four hours later the cow was eating and back to normal). The farmer's wife came out just before I left and said our secretary had telephoned to say that a cow was having difficulty in calving at another farm nearby, so off I went to this case.

'The cow was tied up in a box, the calf's two fore feet had been showing for two hours and seemed to be progressing no further. I put on my calving apron and scrubbed up. I found the calf's head was turned to one side preventing its delivery. It took about ten minutes to bring the head into the normal position and put a rope on to the head to pull it up and forward. A rope was also put on each fore leg and a steady pull by the farmer and his man on these ropes produced a live calf, much to the delight of the farmer who particularly wanted a heifer calf from this cow.

'The calving case finished, it was time to go home and have some lunch.

'14.00 hours saw the start of the afternoon's operations—it being one of our regular operation days. The first case was a female cat to be spayed (womb and ovaries removed to prevent her breeding). She was anaesthetised by administering fluothane and oxygen through a mask over the face. The operation is quite quickly performed through a small incision in the flank, which required three stitches in the abdominal muscles and three in the skin.

'The second case was an old bitch discharging pus from her womb. This is a disease called pyometra. The dog was very ill and had been vomiting a lot. Saline injections had been given to restore her tissue fluids to their normal state. The next step was to remove the womb and ovaries. The dog had been sedated and was then given fluothane and oxygen through a mask until anaesthetised. A tube was then put down into the trachea and connected directly to the anaesthetic machine. The womb was very distended with pus and was carefully removed through a large incision in the abdominal wall after tying off the major blood vessels. The muscles and skin were then sutured up and the anaesthetic turned off. The dog was watched until consciousness returned.

'Finally, I had to put a steel pin in the fractured femur of an Alsatian. The leg had been X-rayed, so I knew the position and type of fracture and could estimate the size of pin needed. The thigh was opened and the fractured ends of bone exposed. The steel pin, held in a chuck, was then inserted into the upper half of the bone and drilled through until it protruded near the hip. It was then pushed down into the lower half. The incised muscles were sutured and the skin closed. These cases usually do very well indeed.

'The operations of the afternoon over, it was time to do some paper work in the office, leaving our animal nurses, who are our invaluable help in the hospital, to clean and re-sterilise the instruments and tidy up the operating theatre. After the paper work I went home to tea and a night on duty.

'That night I had a call to a cow which had milk fever, a complaint in which a newly calved cow goes into a state of paralysis and eventually becomes recumbent due to a fall in calcium in the blood stream. An intravenous injection of calcium solution and a supportive one under the skin soon revived her. In about ten minutes she was on her feet again.

'I was fortunate that this was the only case and so I went to bed at a reasonable hour.

'The telephone woke me at 06.00 hours. This was to see a sow which had been trying to farrow most of the night. The patient was in a pleasantly warm, clean pen and was lying on her side straining at frequent intervals. I asked for warm water, soap and towel, and having cleaned my arm inserted it into the sow's uterus, and found a very large piglet which the sow could not expel. I extracted this piglet and gave an injection of pituitrin. Within the next ten minutes two more piglets arrived naturally, so having cleaned myself up and given an antibiotic injection I left the sow to farrow on her own, unless any more obstructions should occur when I was to be called again.

'Home to breakfast after this, and then off to the surgery for another day, but an evening off duty to follow it.'

David Jemson sums up his life as a veterinary surgeon by saying, 'It still seems to me that after sixteen years in general practice, having suffered triumph and joy, worries, discomfort provided by the weather, frustration and exhaustion, one element is absent and that is boredom, and that is worth a lot to anybody.'

THE ROYAL ARMY VETERINARY CORPS

The Royal Army Veterinary Corps offers an active career for the young veterinary surgeon just down from college; a short service commission can be recommended for the graduate who would like to look around a bit before settling down into general practice. In the main, the veterinary officer deals with dogs, horses and mules. This specialisation can be a valuable asset if he returns to civilian life.

As in all careers in the services, whether regular or short service, there are plenty of opportunities for travel, sport and action. Added to this, the veterinary officer enjoys leave on a scale which few civilians can contemplate—an annual paid leave of up to forty-two days.

Laboratory facilities, drugs, and hospitals are often the most up to date available. Opportunities for research, and publication of findings, are provided and encouraged.

The leaflet *A Career for Regular and Short Service Commissioned Officers in the RAVC*, published by the Central Office of Information, states:

> Whether or not the Veterinary Officer elects to stay in the army at the end of his three-year commission, the veterinarian can't lose. If he decides to return to civilian life, he does so with enhanced professional standing and with a tax-free gratuity

which will help him to set up in private practice should he so wish. If he stays in the Army, he has a head start in the promotion stakes.

Should the veterinary graduate decide to take advantage of the opportunities offered as a veterinary officer on short service commission, he is advised to write to the Army Veterinary and Remount Services, the Ministry of Defence, Droitwich, Worcestershire.

CHAPTER SEVEN

Nursing Auxiliaries

The scope of work open to animal nursing auxiliaries may become wider in future but at present the great majority of them are employed by veterinary surgeons in small-animal practice. The opportunities for male auxiliaries are limited.

In 1961 the Council of the Royal College of Veterinary Surgeons introduced a scheme for the recruitment, training and registration of animal nursing auxiliaries. It was thus made possible for a young person to undergo training to become a registered animal nurse and so pursue a career assisting a veterinary surgeon.

Miss Mary Collins, who works for a veterinary practice in North London, has contributed her personal account of the duties of a Registered Animal Nursing Auxiliary:

The majority of RANA's are employed in small-animal practice, dealing mainly with pet animals ranging from dogs to mice. There are, however, some practices where one may be able to assist on farms with cattle, sheep, pigs and horses. The scope of the work always depends on the size of the practice or hospital concerned.

All of the duties performed by a RANA must be done in an intelligent and responsible manner. Answering the telephone, taking messages, making appointments, answering small queries, possibly giving reports on animals hospitalised, all these require, from the ethical standpoint, careful and sometimes sympathetic handling.

It is important to keep careful records of all patients' ailments and treatments, and to ensure that these are kept up to date and filed in an orderly fashion. Imagine the consternation which would arise if a Siamese stud cat, admitted to the surgery for dental treatment, were confused with a ginger tom that had been booked in for castration!

Whether routine or emergency, operations are performed almost daily. Prior to surgery, the RANA is responsible for preparing the patient, the theatre, the sterilisation of surgical equipment, the anaesthetic apparatus, as well as other requirements for the specific cases of the day. During an operation, anaesthesia is induced by the veterinary surgeon, but is maintained by the RANA who keeps him informed of any respiratory changes. During the majority of operations the veterinary surgeon requires assistance, so with experience the RANA can be of invaluable help.

Radiography is carried out at most veterinary practices, and the task of taking X-rays and developing them is frequently given to the RANA. This can be a very interesting and absorbing job, requiring a good deal of skill in order to obtain the best results.

Any hospitalised animal usually comes under the RANA's care. Accurate daily reports for each animal undergoing treatment and convalescence have to be presented to the veterinary surgeon, and any instructions from him have to be carried out carefully and in a professional manner. It is always important to remember that the animals undergoing treatment rely entirely on the people looking after them for their successful recuperation. Any change in behaviour and appetite has to be included in the daily report submitted to the veterinary surgeon.

The animals' accommodation has to be cleaned out at regular intervals. Grooming, bathing—if an animal's condition permits—

and generally providing as much encouragement as possible, are all essential for the patient's welfare.

Being a RANA entails considerable responsibility in the day-to-day management of a veterinary practice. Animal nursing can undoubtedly be an extremely interesting and rewarding career. However, anyone contemplating embarking on the two-year course is advised, if at all possible, to spend a short time working in a veterinary practice or hospital in order to see exactly the type of work that is entailed in such a career.

ANIMAL NURSING AUXILIARIES SCHEME

The qualifications required by a candidate embarking on this scheme are included in the RCVS booklet *Animal Nursing Auxiliaries—A Guide for Persons Wishing to Train as Registered Animal Nursing Auxiliaries*.

No person may enter for the preliminary examination unless he has been enrolled as a trainee by the Royal College of Veterinary Surgeons and he may not be so enrolled unless he has:

(a) obtained three passes at GCE 'O' level or at CSE Grade 1 level, which shall include a pass in English language and a pass in either a physical or biological science or mathematics; (provided that equivalent passes in comparable examinations in Scotland, Ireland or any other country may be accepted by the Committee in lieu of the foregoing requirements)

(b) reached the age of 17 years;

(c) obtained, in the case of an applicant who has not yet reached the age of 18 years, the consent of his parent or guardian to his enrolment; and

(d) obtained full-time gainful employment of not less than 35 hours per week, or the promise in writing of such employment, at an approved training centre.

APPROVED TRAINING CENTRES

An approved training centre refers to a veterinary practice or other veterinary centre approved by the Committee as possessing adequate facilities for the training of animal nursing auxiliaries, including facilities for modern operative procedures, sideroom tests and hospitalisation or post-operative treatment, or an educational institute approved by the Committee at which full-time courses of instruction for animal nursing auxiliaries are provided.

In a number of areas, local education authorities are providing part-time courses of theoretical instruction to supplement the required practical training at approved training centres. The Royal College of Veterinary Surgeons welcomes this development but enrolment in such a course does not of itself constitute enrolment as a trainee under the scheme.

The RCVS cannot assist people wishing to take up this career to find employment at approved training centres, though it will supply a list of these free on request, and will provide information about a scheme run jointly by the British Small Animal Veterinary Association and the British Animal Nursing Auxiliaries Association to maintain a list of vacancies for trainees. Any veterinary practice or veterinary hospital may apply to the Royal College of Veterinary Surgeons for approval as a training centre; approval is granted if certain conditions are fulfilled. Pay during training and after qualification is a matter for settlement between employer and employee and may vary considerably according to size of practice or veterinary hospital and the geographical location; the Royal College has no jurisdiction in this matter.

PRELIMINARY EXAMINATION

Any person who has been enrolled as a trainee may, at any time thereafter, enter for the preliminary examination whenever such examination is due to be held.

The Committee shall have power to declare that entries for any particular preliminary examination shall be restricted to such trainees or classes of trainees as the Committee may determine, provided always that in the course of each calendar year there shall be at least one preliminary examination which shall be open to all trainees.

The subject matter for both examinations deals mainly with the dog and the cat, but some knowledge is required about the general management of other animals, for example, cage birds, rabbits, hamsters, guinea pigs, mice and tortoises. The fundamental subjects of anatomy and physiology are taken at elementary level and are concerned solely with the dog and the cat.

FINAL EXAMINATION

No trainee may enter for the final examination unless:

(a) he shall have passed the preliminary examination; and
(b) either the period between the date on which he successfully sat the preliminary examination and the date scheduled for the holding of the final examination will be not less than nine months, or, if the period will be shorter than nine months, he has obtained the permission of the Committee to enter for the final examination.

The Committee shall have power to declare that entries for any particular final examination shall be restricted to such trainees or classes of trainees as the Committee may determine, provided always that in the course of each calendar year there shall be at least one final examination which shall be open to all trainees.

RESIDENTIAL COURSES

The following full-time residential courses are held at the Berkshire College of Agriculture:

(a) A six-month (two-term) course from September to March. This course covers the preliminary and final ANA syllabuses. Trainees on the course take their preliminary ANA examination in December, and the final ANA examination in the following July.

(b) A three-month (one-term) course from April to July, on the final ANA syllabus.

Entry to the course is limited to trainees who will, by the time of the commencement of the course, have completed about twelve months' training in approved training centres since enrolment with the RCVS.

Attendance at a course counts as part of a trainee's two-year period of training. At the end of a course a trainee may need to find further employment in an approved training centre in order to complete the required period of two years' training from date of enrolment with the RCVS. The RCVS recognises that some approved training centres may require trainees to terminate their employment on entry to the course, although others may enter into an agreement to re-employ their trainees after they have completed the course. This is entirely a matter for agreement between centres and trainees and the RCVS has no power to intervene.

Trainees will be required to make formal application for entry to these courses and will be notified of the result of their application several months before the commencement of the course. Those interested should write to the Principal, Berkshire College of Agriculture, Hall Place, Burchetts Green, Nr Maidenhead, Berkshire, for full information and details of the courses and of the grants available from local education authorities. As a general rule, the Berkshire College will deal in the preceding January with firm applications to enter the six-month course starting each September. Firm applications to enter the three-month course starting each April will normally be dealt with in the preceding October/November.

CERTIFICATE OF REGISTRATION

The Royal Veterinary College grants a certificate of registration as an animal nursing auxiliary to those who have passed the preliminary and final examination and completed two years' training at an approved training centre since the date of enrolment as a trainee.

The period of two years' training, which need not be continuous, shall be spent in full-time gainful employment of not less than 35 hours per week, at an approved training centre or centres, or in receiving full-time training at an approved educational institute.

Every holder of the certificate of registration may signify the fact of his or her registration with the College as an animal nursing auxiliary by the assumption of the letters RANA after their name.

GENERAL INFORMATION

Fees payable are: trainee enrolment £2.10; each examination £3.15; entry to ANA register £5.25.

The syllabuses for both the preliminary and final examinations are set out in full in the *Guide for Animal Nursing Auxiliaries*, published by the Royal College of Veterinary Surgeons, 32 Belgrave Square, London SW1X 8QP.

Examination papers set for ANA examinations held from 1963 to December 1970 have been collected and printed in a booklet which may be obtained from the Royal College. Papers set and used at subsequent examinations are also available.

Local Youth Employment Officers will be glad to help and advise young people interested in this career.

CHAPTER EIGHT

Animal Technicians

Animal technicians are employed by a wide range of organisations—health services, universities, pharmaceutical firms, agricultural research organisations, veterinary hospitals, zoos and wildlife establishments; however, their main function is working in Home Office registered establishments and large-scale commercial breeding firms.

The type of work ranges through routine care and maintenance of animals, general research assistance, production and specialised breeding, surgical operations (eg nephrectomy)—in fact, the whole spectrum of animal usage. Animal technicians are not allowed to treat animals outside their registered establishments for a fee, as this encroaches on the veterinary profession.

Anyone starting off on this career is usually employed as a junior technician; it is then advisable for him to enrol as a student member of the Institute of Animal Technicians, which runs examinations at three levels: preliminary, associateship and fellowship—the only accepted qualifications in this field.

For information about the IAT examination syllabuses, I am indebted to Mr George Thomson, FIAT, Education Officer, the Education Committee of the IAT.

PRELIMINARY EXAMINATION

The preliminary examination may be attempted by candidates who are employed in an approved establishment and

(a) have had not less than two years' experience in the care of laboratory animals, or

(b) have had not less than one year's experience in the care of laboratory animals and hold:

1 GCE at 'O' level or CSE Grade 1 or the equivalent in English language and one of the following: biology, human physiology or zoology;

or 2 GCE at 'A' level or the equivalent in two subjects, one of which must be a science subject;

or 3 ONC or HNC in applied biology or any other science subject approved by the examination board.

Holders of the national diploma in agriculture or dairying or poultry husbandry or equivalent qualifications and those who are Registered Animal Nursing Auxiliaries are exempted from the preliminary examination.

It is now essential for students to work in registered animal units in order to gain entry to courses and examinations. College courses are also compulsory, and pass results have to be realised before entry to IAT examinations is permitted, although exemptions can be granted under certain conditions. Whilst working at a registered animal unit, the candidate attends a technical college course for one day a week over a period of two years in order to benefit from a total of 140–50 hours of tuition.

The following syllabus (January 1972) for the preliminary examination of the Institute of Animal Technicians illustrates the subjects covered in the first two years of training:

1 Elementary mammalian anatomy and the basic principles of physiology, with special reference to the rat and the rabbit: circulatory system, including structure and functions of the blood; respiratory system; digestive system, urogenital system.

2 Simple arithmetic: conversions between the metric and other

systems in common use; an understanding of the Centigrade and Fahrenheit scales and conversions between the two scales; simple thermometry, to include the maximum-minimum and clinical thermometers; bimetallic strips; thermocouples; calculation of percentages; simple proportion; measurement of area and volume; preparation of solutions of known strength; simple costing of foodstuffs.

3 The Cruelty to Animals Act, 1876: an understanding of the legal requirements covering the management of experimental animals; licences and certificates; the conditions attached to every licence; administration of the Act, including visits of Home Office inspectors; recording of experiments; visitors to experimental areas.

4 Hygiene: disposal of used bedding and carcases; personal hygiene; methods of sterilisation: principles and use of washing machines; free-steam chests; autoclaves; hot air ovens; classification and use of disinfectants; use of fumigants; checks for efficiency of sterilisation processes, eg Browne's tubes; autoclave tape; spore strip.

5 Nutrition: body composition of mammals; major and minor nutrients and their sources; chemical composition of protein, carbohydrate and fat; functions of protein, carbohydrate, fat, minerals and accessory food factors; special reference to the need for a dietary source of vitamin C for the guinea-pig and monkey; diets suitable for the common species, including foodstuffs which could be used in an emergency; correct storage of foodstuffs; detection of deterioration and infestation of foodstuffs.

6 Handling and sexing of common laboratory animals: mouse, rat, guinea-pig, rabbit, Syrian hamster, ferret, cat and dog. NB: When handling an animal candidates should also be able to give an indication of the animal's age and body weight.

7 Routine care of common species and of the Rhesus monkey: methods of feeding and watering; bedding and nesting materials; cleaning of cages, equipment and premises; environmental temperature and humidity, and the optima recommended for various species; inspection for injuries, including sore hocks and overgrown teeth and claws; normal body temperatures.

8 Ill-health in the common species: an elementary knowledge of the causes of ill-health; recognition of the signs of ill-health, eg loss of condition, respiratory infections, infestations.

9 Breeding of the common species: recognition of good breeding animals; elementary knowledge of oestrous cycles; gestation periods; average litter sizes; average birth, weaning and adult body weights;

selection of good breeding stock; duration of economic breeding life; breeding systems: matings at post-partum oestrus, monogamous pairs and harems; closed colonies; inbreeding and random breeding.

10 Methods of identification for common species.

11 Euthanasia for common species.

12 The use and care of animal and food balances: elementary principles of spring, beam and torsion balances.

The preliminary examination consists of written, oral and practical examinations. The written examination takes not less than two hours; the oral and practical not less than thirty minutes. Both sections are held in London and in provincial centres. The provincial venues cannot be decided until after the closing date for registration, when the geographical distribution of candidates is known. All candidates are required to attend both sections of the examination.

ASSOCIATESHIP EXAMINATION

The associateship examination may be attempted by candidates who are employed in an approved establishment and hold the national diploma in agriculture or dairying or poultry husbandry or equivalent qualification or are Registered Animal Nursing Auxiliaries with not less than two years' experience in the care of laboratory animals, or (a) are employed in an approved establishment and hold the preliminary certificate and have had a further two-year course with a total of 350–400 hours of tuition and have had not less than four years' experience in the care of laboratory animals, or (b) have had not less than three years' experience in the care of laboratory animals and hold the GCE at 'O' level or CSE Grade 1 or the equivalent in English language and biology or human physiology or zoology.

For further exemptions, the rules and conditions of IAT examinations and the three examination syllabuses can be obtained in full from the IAT Education Officer.

The main subjects included in the associateship syllabus are: mammalian anatomy and physiology; elementary microbiology;

the Cruelty to Animals Act, 1876; nutrition; hygiene; disease and infestation; management of isolation units for infective animals; manipulations and techniques; breeding of laboratory animals; farm animals used in the laboratory; other species; SPF techniques; animal house equipment; animal house management; subjects covered by the preliminary syllabus but not specified in this syllabus.

The written and practical sections of the associateship examination are held in London and provincial centres. Only candidates who obtain a sufficient aggregate mark in these sections are called for the oral examinations. Candidates may expect to receive about a fortnight's notice telling them whether or not to attend the oral examination. The oral examinations are held regularly in London and will be held in provincial centres whenever the geographical distribution of candidates makes this practicable.

FELLOWSHIP EXAMINATION

The fellowship examination may be attempted by candidates who are employed in an approved establishment and have held the associateship diploma or the certificate of practical ability and competence in specialised techniques for at least two years, and during this time attended a course and undergone some 600 hours of tuition (normally one full day and evening a week), or candidates who were accepted as fellows at the foundation of the Institute of Animal Technicians in 1950.

The main subjects included in the fellowship syllabus are: general anatomy and physiology of laboratory animals, with special reference to mammals and birds; laws relating to the use of laboratory and farm animals; nutrition; elementary genetics; disease; production and management of gnotobiotes; radioactivity in animal experiments; general knowledge of the budgerigar, canary, pigeon, goldfish, trout, newt, salamander and grass snake; animal house design; administration; first aid for laboratory hazards; subjects covered by the preliminary and associateship syllabuses but not specified in this syllabus.

The written sections of the fellowship examinations are held in London and provincial centres. Only candidates who obtain sufficient marks at the written sections are called for the oral and practical examinations; candidates may expect to receive about a fortnight's notice telling them whether or not to attend. The oral and practical examinations are held regularly in London.

GENERAL INFORMATION

Candidates are advised that the handling and sexing of laboratory animals is a compulsory section at all levels of examination. Those who do not attain 75 per cent or more marks in this section automatically fail the whole examination. The pass-mark for other sections of the examination is 50 per cent.

The examination fee for the first and any subsequent re-examination has recently been increased by 50 per cent, the fees are now: £3.00 for preliminary examination; £7.50 for associateship examination; £12.00 for certificate of practical ability and competence in specialised techniques; £12.00 for fellowship examination; £30.00 for fellowship thesis.

For an up-to-date list of where Institute of Animal Technician courses are normally held, and for advice on appointments, candidates should write to the IAT Registered Office, 16 Beaumont Street, Oxford OX1 2LZ.

For current examination forms, prospective candidates should apply individually in writing to the appropriate examination registrar. Names and addresses of registrars can be obtained from the IAT Registered Office or from the current edition of the *Journal of the Institute of Animal Technicians*, which also gives a full list of names and addresses of the IAT officers, branch secretaries, members of the examination board and education committee. Branches of the Institute are established throughout the United Kingdom, providing facilities for members to meet and discuss animal husbandry, and scientific development, and for lectures on relevant topics. An annual congress is arranged, and members are encouraged to contribute original articles to the quarterly journal.

BIOLOGICAL RESEARCH

I am grateful to Mr W. R. Kingston, chief animal technician of a large research station belonging to a well-known pharmaceutical firm, for his first-hand appraisal of a career in this field:

Employment as an animal technician in biological research undoubtedly offers the opportunity to be actively engaged in the care of animals of quite a wide range of species; at the same time salaries compare quite well with other professions, as distinct from zoos, kennels, stables etc, which by and large pay rather badly. However, a special dichotomy of attitude is required in that, although it is necessary to have a real interest and feeling for the animals in order to do the job satisfactorily, you are ultimately faced with the certain knowledge that they will be used in experimental work which always ends in their being put down. If you can face up to this fact and feel convinced that their use in this way is justifiable in terms of alleviation of human health problems, then the job is very satisfying.

As regards the nature of the work, the normal progression for a person starting in their teens is broadly as follows: Your first job is usually as a junior technician and the day's work will consist of the feeding, watering and cleaning out of a room of rats, mice or other species under the supervision of a senior person.

With this groundwork of practical experience and after studying for the IAT preliminary examination (see page 98), you would normally expect to become an animal technician and, depending on the nature of the establishment, progress to being in charge of a room or rooms of either breeding or experimental animals. Some organisations buy all their animals from commercial sources, in which case the work entails only the care of these and a degree of involvement in the experimental procedures, such as holding for injections or oral dosing. Really good observation of the animals to detect signs of ill-health or effects of experimental procedures is essential for this work. If an organisation breeds its own animal requirements, the work will entail mating, checking for pregnancy, assistance with parturition of the larger species, recording of birth and losses, weaning, arranging for a supply of replacement breeders, and the keeping of accurate breeding performance records.

The next stage is to become a senior technician, who will normally be expected to have passed the IAT associate examination and therefore have a good basic knowledge of the anatomy, physiology, reproduction, diseases and general biology of all the usual laboratory species. If breeding is done, you would expect to be responsible for the production of one species, with a suitable staff of junior technicians under your control. This can be quite a responsible job since some institutions breed literally thousands of rats and mice and hundreds of rabbits and guinea pigs weekly, and as many as a thousand dogs and cats annually. Since research depends on these animals for all its work, a breakdown in output can be a very serious matter and planning to avoid such a contingency requires much thought. At this level the work becomes largely supervisory and administrative, earning at present-day scales around £1,500 to £2,000 per annum.

The final stage is a chief technician or animal supervisor, for which a fellowship of the IAT is usually required and which will carry a salary of £2,500 to £4,000 per annum, according to the size of the unit. This work is administrative and will include selection of staff, training programmes, ordering of supplies, responsibility for costings, design and planning of new units and extensions, and acting as a general walking encyclopedia on all animal matters for one's own staff and everyone else up to senior executive level. It is a taxing but rewarding job, comparing in status and remuneration with managers in manufacturing concerns and, with aptitude and application, can be achieved by the age of thirty. It has the advantage of being a relatively uncrowded profession, where the demand exceeds the supply, and is likely to remain so because of the special characteristics required. On the other hand, throughout the whole career strata, it must be realised that one is concerned with living creatures which cannot be turned off like a machine. They need attention seven days a week and will have young or become ill just as often at 3 am on Christmas morning as at any other time. The good animal technician at any level will put the well-being of his charges before anything else, including his own convenience; unless one is prepared to do this, the job is not to be recommended.

TAIL-PIECE

Before concluding this chapter on animal technicians, I would like to briefly put on record the fact that Mr Kingston's work with the maintenance and breeding of colonies of the diminutive South American primate family, Callithricidae (marmosets and tamarins), is well known internationally. Although restricted due to the main objectives behind the majority of pharmaceutical animal research laboratories, during the last decade Mr Kingston has managed to publish more useful data and achieve greater breeding results than any other place in the United Kingdom. It is to some degree thanks to the knowledge collected and recorded by Mr Kingston that there is now a good potential for successfully establishing in captivity self-sustaining breeding groups of a number of this specialised primate family, and by so doing in some cases aiding the survival of a species.

CHAPTER NINE

Nature Conservation and Animal Welfare

If the amount of mail received by Gerald Durrell's Jersey Wildlife Preservation Trust is anything to go by, an increasing number of people are anxious to involve themselves directly in working for animal conservation.

Whereas in pre-war and early post-war days it was comparatively easy to gain employment with a game or wildlife department in one of Britain's colonial possessions, especially in Africa, today these newly independent countries confine the recruitment of game wardens to their own people. A school-leaver's ambition to become a 'legendary white hunter' is thus unlikely to be fulfilled and it must be recognised that the chances of embarking on a career with animals in the wild is now almost impossible. However, there are a number of openings for young people wishing to involve themselves with animals in their natural environment—even if only indirectly.

THE NATURE CONSERVANCY

The Nature Conservancy was established in 1949 to advise on nature conservation, to establish and manage nature reserves, and to carry out research. On 1 June 1965 the Natural Environment Research Council was set up, under whose aegis the Conservancy's activities now continue.

Miss B. Mason, of the Conservancy's recruitment section, has supplied the following details about the organisation's work and the opportunities for employment:

The Nature Conservancy anticipates many conservation problems posed by modern progress. Its advice on these problems is derived partly from its own research, partly from its contact with the work of others in many parts of the world and partly from experiments in different types of management or treatment. Much of this work is carried out on national nature reserves and on other areas of scientific interest.

These reserves are thus not only living museums but outdoor laboratories in which many hundreds of investigations and tests are continuously carried out and checked. In this work Conservancy scientists are reinforced by independent professional and amateur research workers, to whom facilities are given.

The reserves are managed under comprehensive and detailed long-term management plans which take account of many scientific and other factors. National nature reserves cannot be acquired by another public authority and are thereby safeguarded for research.

The Nature Conservancy employs a wide variety of staff, including biologists, geologists, physiographers, land agents, librarians, cartographers, reserve wardens, deer stalkers and estate workers, as well as clerical, executive and administrative staff.

Many of the Conservancy's staff are scientifically trained. Although most of these have graduated in botany or zoology, candidates with degrees in other subjects, eg geography, geology, chemistry or mathematics, are suitable for some posts. A knowledge of birds is found useful by many scientists and wardens, but there are few openings for trained ornithologists because most ornithological tasks are contracted out to specialist bodies.

Many of the scientific staff are working on fundamental research in research stations or field stations, and the remainder are employed on regional work throughout Great Britain in the conservation branch. Duties of conservation branch staff include the management of nature reserves and some related research; the giving of advice on the protection of sites of special scientific interest and on general conservation problems, as well as maintaining close liaison with public bodies, naturalists' trusts and landowners.

Scientific appointments are made initially either to the conservation branch or to a specific research team, but as these two aspects of the Conservancy's work are closely associated, staff may move from one to the other.

Reserve wardens

Through their regional officer, wardens are responsible for the implementation of management plans, scientific recording and other matters concerning the welfare of national nature reserves. One warden may be responsible for several reserves, or more than one warden may be employed on the same reserve.

Candidates should be not less than twenty-six years of age, and must be keen naturalists and interested in field studies. They should be able to drive and maintain vehicles, and have some practical knowledge of estate management.

The duties of a warden include making defined scientific observations in relation to scientific problems, with a minimum of supervision; writing reports and maintaining daily records, and giving talks to local bodies on the purpose and work of his reserve. He must be able to supervise all regular types of estate work, with assistance of casual or other labour as appropriate, and to carry this out himself when such assistance is not available. The warden's relations with the public and with neighbouring landowners and occupiers require tact and understanding.

The posts are filled by annual competition usually announced in the spring. The competition is run in conjunction with the Civil Service Commission and is advertised in the national newspapers and such journals as *Nature* and the *New Scientist*.

Appointments to the warden class are made to the reserve warden grade. There are opportunities for promotion to senior warden and chief warden grades on the basis of capacity, experience and responsibilities.

Wardens are required to serve a trial period of not less than two years from the date of appointment, after which they may be nominated to the Civil Service Commissioners for an established (ie superannuable) appointment. On establishment they join the Natural Environment Research Council Superannuation Scheme.

The working week for warden grades is forty-five hours, not including lunch hours. There is no payment of overtime and wardens remain liable to work additional hours as required. Time off is allowed for the usual public holidays and for the equivalent of two days weekly.

Conservancy establishments

There are six regional offices for England, three for Scotland and two for Wales. More than sixty full-time wardens and many honorary and part-time wardens and estate workers work on the national nature reserves.

ENGLAND

Furzebrook Research Station, Wareham, Dorset

Ecology of lowland heathlands including primary and secondary production, nutrient budgets, litter decomposition and invertebrate populations.

Merlewood Research Station, Grange-over-Sands, Lancashire

Research into natural and semi-natural woodland ecosystems; including site classification, monitoring of changes, dynamics, taxonomic and biological variation of plants and animals. Research into biological activity in the soil, particularly woodland and moorland soils. Studies of individual organisms believed to be important in defined ecosystems. Development of mathematical models of ecosystems. Provision of service of analytical chemistry, together with development of analytical techniques and maintenance of a data bank of analytical results. (Also regional office for North of England.)

Moor House Field Station, Carrigill, Alston, Cumberland
Upland ecology and conservation studies.

Monks Wood Experimental Station, Abbots Ripton, Huntingdon
Effects of pesticides and other pollutants on plants and animals. Ecology and conservation of vertebrate and invertebrate species in the lowlands. Ecology and management of lowland grassland and grass heaths. Woodland survey and management. Recording of biological data.

Foxhold House, Thornford Road, Crookham Common, near Newbury, Berkshire
Geographical and physiographic conservation. (Also regional office for the South of England.)

Coastal Ecology Research Station, Colney Lane, Norwich NOR 7OF
Research on mudflats, saltmarshes, shingle beaches, dune systems and cliffs. Studies and the environmental factors controlling them.

Other regional offices are at Attingham Park, Shrewsbury, Shropshire (Midland Region); 60 Bracondale, Norwich NOR 58B (East Anglia Region); Roughmoor, Bishops Hull, Taunton, Somerset (South-West Region) and Zealds, Church Street, Wye, Ashford, Kent (South-East Region). There are also a number of regional sub-offices.

SCOTLAND

Headquarters for Scotland: 12 Hope Terrace, Edinburgh EH9 2AS

Ecology of wetlands, especially Loch Leven. Mountain and moorland ecology especially herbivore vegetation interactions. Conservation. (Regional offices for all Scottish regions.)

Mountain and Moorland Habitat Team, Blackhall, Banchory, Kincardineshire

Mountain and moorland ecology, especially concerning red grouse, ptarmigan and other birds and the interaction between red deer and their vegetation. Studies of human impact in the Cairngorms.

WALES

Headquarters for Wales and Bangor Research Station, Penrhos Road, Bangor, Caernarvonshire

Montane Grassland Habitat Team: Ecology and land use conservation in western upland Britain.

Pedology Section: Field, chemical, physical and mineralogical aspect of soil science applied to ecology and conservation in Britain.

Director's Laboratory: Relationship between grassland vegetation production and sheep grazing.

Conservancy contacts and collaboration

Work with the Nature Conservancy provides the candidate, especially the university graduate, with a promising career involving teamwork in research, information, education and conservation.

The Conservancy keeps in touch with most of those interested in natural history and nature conservation in Britain and overseas. These include botanists, entomologists, wildfowl conservationists, geologists, educators in field studies, nature photographers and other kindred interests. These co-operate with the Conservancy through a network of liaison committees where information and views are exchanged, objectives agreed and any differences resolved at national level.

In Britain nearly all voluntary bodies in the field of conservation are linked with one another and with the Nature Conservancy through the Council for Nature (founded 1958), several of whose officers have also served in a personal capacity on the Conservancy.

In most English and Welsh counties local naturalists participate in conservation through the naturalists' trusts with which regional officers of the Conservancy co-operate very closely. Several of the leaders of this movement also serve on Conservancy committees. The trusts themselves are also linked nationally with the Conservancy through the Society for the Promotion of Nature Reserves.

Contacts are also maintained with most British universities, and at many of these certain work is grant-aided or otherwise supported.

On the international plane, the Conservancy maintains close contacts with the International Union for Conservation of Nature and Natural Resources (IUCN), the World Wildlife Fund, the International Council for Bird Preservation, the International Wildfowl Research Bureau, the Council of Europe and many overseas bodies, and also with the Ministry of Overseas Development. The Conservancy's part in this many-sided teamwork is internationally appreciated and it contributes to British prestige in many parts of the world.

The Conservancy takes part in the spectacular advances of modern biology, in which ecology is a major growing point; in the analyses and measurement of biological productivity on land, in the tracing of factors regulating animal populations, and in following through the effects of soil and climate on plants and animals. Conservancy scientists form probably the world's largest and most closely knit ecological research team. It is playing a significant part in the International Biological Programme, which is a counterpart to the International Geophysical Year.

FURTHER INFORMATION

Fuller information about the work of the Conservancy is contained in the reports of the Natural Environment Research Council published by HM Stationery Office, Atlantic House, Holborn Viaduct, London EC1. For details about careers in the Nature Conservancy, candidates should write to The Nature Conservancy, 19–20 Belgrave Square, London SW1X 8PY.

Information concerning the thirty-six county naturalists' or conservation trusts, which maintain some 250 nature reserves comprising over 20,000 acres in England, Scotland and Wales, as well as details regarding membership or employment, can be obtained from the Society for the Promotion of Nature Reserves (SPNR), The Manor House, Alford, Lincolnshire.

VOLUNTARY CONSERVATION WORK

Almost everyone can find some opportunity to join in this great world effort for conservation through one or other of the many voluntary bodies linked with the Conservancy.

There are, for instance, many openings for:

Adults to serve as honorary wardens of nature reserves or to help the activities of naturalists' trusts;

Teachers and educationists to take part in the vast educational effort which is now beginning at all levels;

Bird-watchers, botanists, entomologists and other naturalists to fill gaps in information by taking part in surveys through their societies;

All people of goodwill to join one or more bodies of their own choice and to give their time or money to the rewarding aims of conservation.

National Conservation Corps

Young people (especially those aged between sixteen and twenty-three) can learn about and work in wild places by joining the British Trust for Conservation Volunteers which, amongst other projects, carries out tasks on nature reserves and for naturalists' trusts.

In 1973, a group of seventeen Conservation Corps volunteers first came to Jersey for a fortnight and stayed at an old fort situated on the cliffs on the north of the island in order to undertake a project at the Jersey Wildlife Preservation Trust. I have seldom been so impressed as I was by the sense of purpose and team spirit of this group of volunteers in helping, by their own hard work, the conservation objectives of the JWPT (see Chapter Ten). If these Conservation Corps volunteers represent a typical cross-section of public opinion, the conservation of land and water, and of their plant and animal life, would be gratifyingly secure for the benefit of all future generations.

For full particulars of tasks undertaken, would-be volunteers should write to National Conservation Corps, Zoological Gardens, Regent's Park, London NW1 4RY.

THE RSPCA

There are a considerable number of animal charities registered in the British Isles, but few provide a career directly involving animals. The Royal Society for the Prevention of Cruelty to Animals (RSPCA) is one organisation which does offer a rewarding and worthwhile career for anyone wishing to do as much as possible for animals in distress.

RSPCA inspector at work

The type of work that an RSPCA inspector may expect to handle during a twenty-four-hour period is described by Chief Inspector Cyril Heath, who joined the RSPCA as a probationer inspector in September 1952, was appointed inspector in April 1953, and has served in RSPCA stations at Oxford, Stroud, Yeovil, Winchester and Guildford:

'Each working day is different to the one preceding it, and the variety of this work makes it all the more enjoyable. The telephone frequently rings during pre-breakfast hours with news about an animal in distress which needs attention, an unwanted pet, people seeking advice, or wanting to register a complaint. All of these require a courteous and satisfactory reply, and are subsequently dealt with by order of priority during the course of the day.

'The process of getting up is combined with feeding Tinker, the household's fourteen-year-old ginger tom. As a kitten he was found on a cold winter's night abandoned outside the residence of a doctor. Tinker has since been one of the lucky ones, benefiting from an ample daily supply of food and a warm and happy home.

'By 8 am the mail is opened. This is apt to cover topics as varied as those in the previous telephone calls: a letter of complaint about the state of a donkey's hooves; please could a puppy be collected as the owner now has to go out to work; veterinary accounts that have to be checked off and submitted for payment; an inquiry from a young schoolboy who wishes to become an animal defender; an advertisement circular, as well as personal correspondence—all are filed in the appropriate places, some influencing the framework of the day's duties.

'An urgent message received from a mobile police car, relayed by telephone from the local police station—a dog has been involved in an accident on the A3, please will I attend. I find on arrival that the two police officers have removed the injured dog on to a blanket beside the grass verge. With the aid of the radio control (all RSPCA inspectors' vehicles are now on radio, providing a most efficient service) a veterinary surgeon will immediately see the unfortunate animal at his surgery.

'As the animal had no collar, I made inquiries on a nearby housing estate. After a considerable investigation, I finally managed to trace the owner. A strong word of warning to the owner for allowing the dog to wander, then I provided a collar with a disc on it giving the dog's name and address. After veterinary treatment the dog recovered. It was one of the more fortunate.

'Now off into the country to put to sleep an aged sick cat, the property of an old age pensioner. En route, I observe a lorry conveying crates of live chickens, stopped in a lay-by. I pull in and have a look at the load, everything in order, the driver informs me that the chickens are going for killing. A look at my list of calls. Yes, I am near the village where there has been a complaint about a chained-up dog. The person complained of is visited, advice given.

'Passing across the common on the way home, I stop and examine the necks of several ponies which are tethered by chains. No cuts, for the chains around the necks are covered with rags. Owner a gypsy.

'Arriving home for lunch, my wife informs me of the incoming calls. Nothing urgent; if there had been, contact would have been made through the radio system. A young racing pigeon had been brought to the house, as the local racing pigeon secretary was on holiday.

At 1.30 pm more telephone calls: a swan in trouble, a hook with fishing line and float caught in beak, specimen at present in a field, location given. A horse in a thin condition seen by a person travelling on a train. Homes wanted for kittens. Would I be able to judge at a village pet show?

'Leave home by 2 pm. Visit local pet shop to purchase some pigeon mixture. Drive on to location of swan in distress. It was found to be a cob, with a pen and cygnet near at hand. All had now returned to the river. A campaign of capture to be worked out; it was found that the cygnet could be enticed to the river bank with bread, so with the aid of a 'swan grasper' he was easily caught. With the help of a member of the public, the cygnet was held on the bank, which induced the cob and the pen to come right up to the river bank themselves. Whereupon, without much difficulty, the 'swan grasper' repeated its capturing operation; the cob was removed from the water, and the hook and tackle disentangled from the beak. After inspecting to see that the swan was in a satisfactory condition after its ordeal, it was released at the same time as the cygnet. With great satisfaction, I witness the family swim off down river unhindered. This type of peril is caused by careless anglers leaving a ready-baited and unattended line without taking the necessary safety precautions.

'Called on a person who has a problem of a stray half-wild cat and kittens living in a wood at the bottom of the garden. A cat trap cage is left. All the necessary arrangements are made as regards how and when to contact me.

'Proceeding homeward, my last call is at a local boarding kennels and cattery. Arriving home in the region of 5.30 pm, a look at the message pad. Someone has lost their cat, and a missing dog has been found. Feed the pigeon, then tea.

'About 6 pm make a few telephone calls, and receive some incoming ones.

'Will I have a peaceful night? It is 10 pm but still the telephone could call me out. Yes, I did check that my vehicle had sufficient petrol for a long night run. Tomorrow will be different—on duty, all day, in a cattle market.'

London Airport's animal hostel

At the RSPCA Airport Hostel for Animals, Heathrow Airport, London, under the managership of Mr N. H. Whittacker, sixteen female assistants see to the general welfare of the animals throughout the 24-hour period, for the hostel is responsible for the care of all livestock passing through the airport. I personally recall with gratitude the two days I once spent at the hostel with a collection of animals I had brought back from Africa. The attendants could not have done more for their needs.

The 'passengers' range from elephants to ants. Sizeable consignments of pedigree dogs en route to Japan; primates for medical research; tropical birds for commercial avicultural dealers, and tropical fish for aquariums—these have contributed to a total of over 14 million specimens passing through London Airport since the hostel's inception in 1952. Thanks to this dedicated team of animal attendants, who are taken on and trained by the RSPCA for these special duties, the death-rate among livestock during transportation is kept to the minimum.

For details about taking up a career with the RSPCA, anyone interested should write to the Personnel Manager, Royal Society for the Prevention of Cruelty to Animals, The Manor House, Horsham, Sussex RH2 1HG.

CHAPTER TEN

Zoos and Bird Gardens

In January 1974, there were, within the British Isles, seven zoological societies, eleven municipal zoos, seventy-five commercial zoos and thirty-four bird gardens open to the paying public.

The popularity of zoological parks means the growth in the exhibition of exotic animals is likely to continue; and it is my hope that this growth will be matched by an increasing number of dedicated people taking up a career in such institutions. It is also hoped that—when the Control of Zoological Gardens bill becomes law—those zoos which are not run in a professional manner will either hastily improve their standards to the required level or be closed down. Zoological parks are the custodians of some of the rarest animal species left in the world today. If they are going to be of real benefit to the animal kingdom, competent staffing at all levels is essential.

WORKING IN A ZOO

The majority of zoos in the British Isles will employ school leavers as trainee attendants; a few will take trainees at sixteen, while others will not employ animal staff below the age of twenty-one.

At present there is no national training scheme for keepers on the same lines as that for animal nursing auxiliaries and technicians. However, the Federation of Zoological Gardens of Great Britain and Ireland plan to promote one after the Control of Zoological Gardens bill is passed.

Some zoo directors prefer to employ animal staff who have had previous zoo experience, whereas others recruit people with no such background so that they can be moulded into the ways of the establishment concerned.

University graduates are on the increase in entering the zoo profession. Providing they have the ability to apply their academic knowledge in a practical fashion, graduates are frequently offered better positions on the zoo staff than those who join direct from school.

In both categories, there is a training period in order to acclimatise the new staff member to zoo work. Providing the trainee exhibits a degree of enthusiasm and is generally conscientious about the job concerned, a position on the permanent staff is usually guaranteed.

Approximately three-quarters of the people looking after zoo animals in the British Isles are male, but perhaps this is due to tradition rather than to any outstanding quality among male employees. Some zoo directors will argue that the nature of some of the jobs necessitates physical strength and that it is essential to have men in charge of the larger mammals. On the other hand, some have a preference for female staff in looking after small mammals, young anthropoid apes, tropical birds and sick-bays. Looking at the broad spectrum of zoo jobs, there is no reason why any of them cannot be done equally well by men and women, providing the basic interest and enthusiasm are there.

Promotion is naturally based on initiative, taking into consideration the ability of the staff to apply experience in a practical fashion to the general benefit of the animals under their care. It is essential for those in senior positions to keep themselves up to date with the many developments in the field of modern zoo science; they should also possess the quality of being able to instruct and control the staff under them.

The order of promotion and increased responsibility is: trainee-keeper, keeper, head of section, head keeper, assistant curator, curator of mammals, birds, reptiles etc, assistant director, and director.

The weekly working hours rather depend on the size of the zoo; for staff at the larger and old-established zoos may work a shorter basic week than those at some of the smaller and younger concerns.

In an average-sized zoo, a keeper can expect to work a 5½-day week; comprising approximately 46½ hours during the summer months, and 44 hours during the winter. Senior members of the zoo staff must expect to be called at any time of the day or night, and in emergencies are known to work a seven-day week. At the majority of zoos the animal staff have three weeks' holiday a year. Some directors request their staff to take their holiday in two parts, believing this to be of greater benefit to both the zoo and the staff member. Extra time-off may be given when staff request to visit other zoological establishments.

A complete list of addresses and names of senior personnel of the world zoos can be obtained by writing to the Editor, The International Zoo Yearbook, The Zoological Society of London, Regent's Park, London NW1 4RY.

A list of the addresses of British zoos is available from the Secretary, The Federation of Zoological Gardens of Great Britain and Ireland, Zoological Gardens, Regent's Park, London NW1 4RY.

Work with small mammals

David Riordan, BSc, is in charge of the small mammal section at the Jersey Zoological Park, HQ of the Jersey Wildlife Preservation Trust, Les Augrès Manor, Trinity, Jersey, Channel Islands. This is an account of his work with small mammals:

The Jersey Zoo's varied small mammal collection of ninety-three specimens accommodated in forty-three different units consists of the following twenty-four species:

Echidna	Emperor tamarin
Pigmy hedgehog tenrec	Saddle-back tamarin
Spiny hedgehog tenrec	Geoffroy's tamarin
Tailless tenrec	Pinche tamarin
Tree shrew	Red-handed tamarin
Mouse lemur	Sierra Leone striped squirrel
Ring-tailed lemur	Argentine red squirrel
Mongoose lemur	Malabar giant squirrel
Brown lemur	Agouti
Senegal bushbaby	Hutia
Common marmoset	Fennec fox
Black-pencilled marmoset	Dog mongoose

Work at the zoo starts at 08.00 hours. The small mammals are situated in three different locations. All the units have to be cleaned and made presentable by the time the zoo opens to the public at 10.00 hours.

The servicing of each unit involves: checking to see that each animal is in good health; the removal of food dishes, noting the quantity of food left from the previous day in order to establish any falling off of appetite; and observing the amount and consistency of the animal's faeces—both food intake and the condition of the faeces act as the animal's barometer. Each nest box is checked and nesting material replenished where necessary; perches are adjusted, and all dirt removed from unit. Cage temperatures and humidity readings are noted and sometimes altered for increased day readings. Cage locks are checked for security reasons. The public viewing area is swept down.

Before cage servicing can commence the following utensils are collected: long-handled soft brush; hand-brush; hand-shovel; plastic bucket filled with warm water and added disinfectant detergent; rubber window-cleaner for glass fronts of units; cloth and scrubbing brush; plastic waste bin; sack of nesting material.

08.00 The first animals to be serviced are the nocturnal small mammals, which include a large collection of tenrecs (insectivores from Madagascar), mouse lemurs, bushbabies, sugar gliders, hutias, echidnas, Fennec foxes. As these animals would not normally be seen during the daylight hours, daylight lighting is switched on during our night-time, and nocturnal lighting is switched on at 09.00 hours so that the animals are active and can be observed by daytime visitors. The units have to be checked and cleaned in time for this switch over.

09.00 The next part of the section to be serviced is the marmoset and tamarin collection. Special care has to be taken prior to a parturition and during the early stages of an infant marmoset's life. When such cases materialise, woodwool is scattered over the cage floor in order to prevent a pregnant mother or a sibling from harm in the event of a fall.

09.30 The final part of the small mammal section to be serviced is the lemur range. As some adult lemurs become untrustworthy, it is necessary to shut them outside or into their inside accommodation whilst their cages are serviced. Fresh sprigs of tree branches are given at this time.

10.00 Morning break.

10.15 The food dishes are washed, and the daily supply of fresh raw meat—some minced with a carnivorous supplement sprinkled over—is collected from the meat kitchen.

10.40 The diurnal lemurs are the first to be fed. Great care has to be taken not to overfeed the specimens, especially the lemurs which are prone to become overweight and, in doing so, are unlikely to breed. Although a nutritionally balanced diet has been worked out for each species, an animal has its own likes and dislikes, so individual whims have to be catered for. As ring-tailed lemurs are constantly grooming themselves, a laxative has to be administered at frequent intervals in order to combat fur-balls from forming a blockage.

11.15 The marmoset family are the next to be fed. A wide variety of fruit and some vegetables are finely chopped up to a size that can easily be picked up in a marmoset's hand, along with some hard-boiled egg, minced meat, and an omnivorous nut, and a complan/honey/vitamin mixture is prepared. New World primates require a high level of Vitamin D3 in their diet, so before the main feed is given David Riordan has to chop up twenty-five pieces of banana, one for each marmoset and tamarin. To each section of banana a drop of Vit D3 equalling 500iu is added; and then each sliver is hand-fed to ensure that each animal gets its daily supplementation. Once this has been completed, the main food is given.

12.00 The last of the morning feeds is for the nocturnal animals, with their preparation of diced soft fruit, vegetable, minced meat and vitamin mixture. The rodents are given much the same, but with some harder fruits and vegetables added. The Fennec foxes and the dog mongoose are the last to be fed. David Riordan then clears up the mammal kitchen before going off for lunch.

13.00 Lunch break.

14.00 During this time all the small mammals are looked at to ensure that everything is all right.

14.20 Many of the small mammals are weighed weekly and some are also measured to record growth development. The mouse lemurs have not only their weights recorded, but also the condition of the base of their tails, and their breeding condition, in order to establish whether they are ready to mix with a mate. All such mixings are recorded so that gestation periods can be established. This early afternoon period is also used to re-perch or totally renovate some of the cages, for there is seldom time to do this during the tightly scheduled morning.

15.15 The morning feed dishes for the lemurs are removed from the cages and washed, and a small night feed is prepared.

15.30 Afternoon break.

15.45 – 17.00 The previously prepared lemur night-feed is given, after which the remaining small mammals have a variety of night feeds, including dishes of milk, water and vitamin supplements, pink day-old mice, crickets, locusts and meal worms. A final check of cage temperatures is made and any disorder reported.

David Riordan's final task is to write down any observations he has made about the animals under his care in the zoo day diary; every animal in the collection has an individual history, medical, breeding and behaviour card. The following morning, a secretary types any recorded observation on to the respective cards. The data collected during the course of the year is included in a paper which David Riordan is expected to write for the Jersey Wildlife Preservation Trust's annual report.

On a busy summer's day, visiting members of the public ply David Riordan with questions about his wards. Occasionally an animal is sick and has to be coaxed to take a medication. Another which is not considered to be pregnant may suddenly produce some young, whilst others may firmly refuse to reproduce. Whatever the case, David Riordan's day is packed with constant variety and interest.

Work with hoofed mammals

Mr T. B. Kichenside worked with hoofed mammals for some fifteen years before gaining his promotion to head keeper at the Zoological Society of London. The London Zoo is divided into sections, each being the immediate responsibility of one head keeper. The head keeper is responsible for the animals and the staff on the section. His duties range from ordering food and miscellaneous stores to requesting repairs and small alterations to be done, the general husbandry of the stock, as well as public relations at section level.

To apply for the position of head keeper, one must be a senior keeper who has worked with the stock for some time; it also helps to have one or both of the Zoo's diplomas in the care and management of animals. After application one is selected by a committee of senior zoo staff at an interview.

The curator of mammals—who completes the chain from keeper, senior keeper, head keeper, overseer, to curator—plays the major role in the administration and long-term planning of the Zoo's mammal collection.

The mammals that are the head keeper's immediate responsibility number approximately 116 specimens, belonging to twenty-eight different species:

Przwalski's wild horse	Blackbuck
Cape buffalo	Defassa water buck
European bison	Blesbok
American bison	Gnu or brindled wildebeeste
Anoa	Kudu
Yak	Alpaca
Timor deer	Llama
Père David deer	Guanaco
Axis deer	Arabian camel
Fallow deer	Bactrian camel
Turkmenian onager	Sitattunga
Giraffe	Mara
Common zebra	Barbary sheep
Grevy zebra	Red deer

As head keeper in charge of eight men, Mr Kichenside describes his work in the hoofed mammal section at the London Zoo:

'The normal time for starting work is 8 am and the normal finishing time is alternately 4 pm and 6.15 pm, making a 40 hour week. The Zoo closes at 6 pm.

'When on duty, one must be available to answer questions from members of the public, and also patrol the section to make sure that the stock is all right.

'The report sheet is the link between the overseer and the head keeper. It should have all information on births, deaths, works jobs, staff and duties for that day. Sick animals and any other general information are also documented.

'The camels and llamas, which provide the children with rides each afternoon, have to be trained by my section, and we are responsible for leading them as well as looking after them.

'A day's work consists mainly of cleaning and feeding. These jobs have to be done every day including Christmas Day. Next on the list is standing on duty, as it is important to keep the public well informed, looked after and under control (eg to prevent the feeding of stock).

'A typical day's work is as follows:

05.45 Arrive at the Zoo. Make up milk and feed baby Arabian camel and Barbary sheep, after which take baby camel for a walk around the Zoo for exercise. Check all houses for new births and sick or injured animals.

08.15 Write out the report sheet and change for work. Deploy staff in each of the houses and give information on any changes to the daily routine. Check back in report book over last month and make a list of any maintenance jobs not yet completed.

08.45 Assist with the cleaning and feeding of the giraffes and zebras.

10.00 Make up bottles and feed babies.

10.45 Assist with the cleaning and feeding in the deer house.

11.30 Check grain order against duplicate sheet.

12.00 Tea break. Wash, change into uniform for lunch.

13.30 Make up bottles for 2 pm feed.

14.30 Walk down to main square to see if riding animals are working properly. (Most of the riding stock comes from my section, ie llamas and camels).

15.00 Back to section and stand on duty.

16.00 Tea break. After tea, stand on duty until 5 pm. Start to bed down and bring in giraffes, zebras, camels and antelopes.

17.30 It was observed that a yak had started to give birth.

17.45 Close cattle house for the night. Stay behind and observe birth. Mother and baby well. Leave note for the man coming back to feed the babies, asking him to make sure they are all right.

18.45 Go home.

'The above duties form the basis of our work. Hardly a day passes without something out of the ordinary happening—a birth, a new animal arriving, the treatment of a sick animal, or the need to bottle-feed an abandoned baby. Few days in a keeper's or head keeper's life are identical; daily surprises are apt to stimulate and reward all who are making a career working with zoo animals.'

Work with reptiles

For the layman, work with reptiles is not often the first choice of zoo work. In the majority of cases, people are unaware of the beauty and fascination of the reptile kingdom, until they have some first-hand experience with them.

Mr Roger Ainsley has been working with reptiles for over twenty years; since 1970, he has been Curator of Reptiles at the North of England Zoological Society at Chester Zoo.

Roger Ainsley is directly responsible for over 177 specimens belonging to 87 species; a cross-section of these are as follows:

Copperhead snake
Black-necked cobra
Chinese cobra
Pope's pit vipers
Rhino vipers
Gaboon vipers
Puff adder
Russell's viper
Jackson's tree snake
King snake
Chicken snake
Boomslang
Snake-necked terrapin
Stink pot
Giant tortoise
Marginated tortoise
Royal python
Reticulated python
Amethystine python
Cooke's tree boa
Madagascan tree boa
Pacific rattlesnake
Siamese crocodile
Watling Island iguana

Black mamba	Solomon Island skink
Clouded monitor	Stump-tailed skink
Timor monitor	Eyed skink
Freckled monitor	Tuatara
Nile crocodile	Plated lizard
Dwarf crocodile	Bearded lizard
Broad-fronted crocodile	Eastern water dragon
Mata Mata turtle	Gila monster

Roger Ainsley's working day starts at 8 am with a walk around the vivariums to ensure that all the specimens are present and in good health. This check takes place before anyone enters the servicing area at the back of the cages, so that, in the unlikely event that a specimen had escaped, we would not walk in unguardedly. Diets have to be worked out for each species and every day a check is made to establish which reptiles need feeding. Preparation of food and cleaning out of the vivariums are daily tasks. A daily check is also made as to whether any specimens require medical attention.

Cage display and maintenance form another part of the curator's responsibilities. This includes the collection of suitable cage decorations, such as logs and branches; selection and maintenance of plant life; arrangement and construction of rockwork, and painting of the vivarium.

To be a successful keeper, one has to consider both the welfare of the animals and the attractiveness of the exhibit to the public. The first point is of major importance if one is going to be successful in breeding reptiles, and in this respect Chester Zoo has a good record of achievement.

A ZOO'S ROLE IN CONSERVATION

In an attempt to analyse what the familiar word 'zoo' conveys to most people, I have come to the conclusion that the majority have little or no idea as to the type of work that can be carried out for the benefit of the animal kingdom in a well-run zoological institution—apart from fulfilling a basic recreational requirement.

It appears to me that, as far as the function and merit of a zoo is concerned, it really all depends on what the chief objectives are behind its creation. Is the zoo there solely to meet human needs and vested interests, or for the benefit of the animals as well? Only when in possession of these facts, can one weigh up the pros and cons and equate how much a particular zoo can contribute to the breeding of rare and endangered species, to education, and to scientific research, and in these ways to aid the conservation of wildlife.

Management of a species

The problems of establishing viable breeding groups are numerous, and it is essential to consider each species separately in order to understand and provide the optimum conditions under which it should be kept.

The chief requisite for successful breeding is, in the first instance, the rather obvious factor—the possession of a compatible pair; then the provision of a well-balanced diet, good accommodation, and a professional staff to look after them. The human element is of paramount importance in creating conditions in captivity in which the animals can be contented, for without contentment and security there is unlikely to be satisfactory breeding. If the human relationship with the animal is one of interest and sympathy, the animal will thrive; otherwise it will not.

When establishing a species in a zoo, one takes into account any guidelines that may be available on their accommodation and dietary requirements. Once a pair has become compatible in the zoo environment, it is then hoped that the species will successfully propagate. Failing this, one has to investigate further into the whims of the specimens concerned, and by the process of elimination, work out a formula as to their individual management.

By the establishment of viable breeding groups of animals in captivity, one has the opportunity of creating a reservoir of an endangered species. By working towards this objective, a zoo can help to ensure that an animal population becomes secure in captivity. Also, progress will be made towards zoos becoming almost self-supporting, so minimising the drain from dwindling wild populations.

A lot has been said about zoos still being consumers rather than producers of wildlife. With the setting up of zoos and wildlife parks all over the British Isles, which demand instant stocking with animals, the erosion of some species has been greatly accelerated and there has been a lack of sufficiently well-trained personnel. For these reasons all of us directly involved with the management of a collection of exotic species have before us one of the most important and exciting challenges in contributing to the conservation of wildlife—by the breeding of animals in captivity, by education and by scientific research. It is hoped it will not be too long before the formal training scheme for zoo personnel—mentioned earlier—can be arranged, for zoo animals deserve the best calibre of the human race to look after them. It is my hope, too, that the *main* objective of a zoological park will be to ensure that it is run for the benefit of the animal kingdom and not merely for financial gain.

BIRD GARDENS

Sir Peter Scott's Wildfowl Trust, at Slimbridge, is world renowned for its conservation and scientific work, in particular the successful propagation of the once endangered Hawaiian goose. In 1952, there were only forty-two Hawaiian geese known to exist in the world. At that time, three were sent to the Wildfowl Trust, which has since reared 820, returned 200 to the wild, and distributed over 180 birds on loan to forty international zoos and private wildfowl breeders. Thanks to the captive propagation of this species, the Hawaiian goose is no longer listed as an endangered species.

Work with waterfowl

Mr Perry Tucker, a South African who has lived in the United Kingdom for some seven years, has been working for three years with Mr Christopher Marler's well-known and comprehensive bird collection at the Flamingo Park and Tropical Bird Zoo at Olney in Buckinghamshire. After leaving school at the age of eighteen, and before specialising in the maintenance and breeding of waterfowl, Perry Tucker attended a three-year course at an agricultural college where he obtained a national diploma. For as long as he can remember, he has been a lover of all species of birds, with his particular favourites belonging to the Anatidae, the waterfowl family.

The bird garden has approximately forty acres of enclosures set aside from the rest of the zoo and not open to the public. The waterfowl under Perry Tucker's care number approximately 550 specimens. These consist of forty-three swans belonging to ten species; 366 geese belonging to forty-two species, and 146 ducks belonging to forty-three species. The following species are represented:

SWANS	GEESE
Whooper	Emperor
Bewick's	Red-breasted
Black	Ross's
Trumpeter	Pink-footed
Black-necked	Western bean
Coscoroba	Thick-billed bean
Whistling	Black spurwing
Jankowsi's	Magpie
Polish	Abyssinian blue-winged
Mute	Dusky Canada
	Vancouver Canada
	Hawaiian
	Andean
	Cereopsis

DUCKS	Chestnut crested duck
Chiloe wigeon	Falcated teal
Cape teal	Brazilian teal
Atlantic blue-winged teal	Australian shelduck
Patagonian crested duck	Cuban whistling duck

Perry Tucker gives this personal account of his work with waterfowl:

'Out of the breeding season, my work commences at 8 am. I start the day by feeding wheat and turkey breeder pellets to the entire collection, and at the same time taking the opportunity to see that all the birds are healthy and in their right pens—particularly the more aggressive species which have to be isolated in pairs in their own specific pens, divided by 4ft wire-netting fences.

'On a normal day it takes approximately two hours to feed the entire collection. The birds are fed once a day, with the exception of the eider ducks which need feeding twice daily. They receive breeder pellets and Purina dog biscuits as they require a high-protein diet.

'After the feeding is completed, I commence maintenance work—for example, repairing leaks in pools, cutting grass to keep it palatable, and constructing temporary internal wire-netting fences—also catching young birds to be exhibited at the zoo and returning potential breeding birds from the zoo to the breeding grounds.

'Once the breeding season is complete, a lot of my time is taken up by hatching bantam eggs in incubators, as well as under hens. We breed as many bantams as possible so that we always have sufficient broody hens to sit on clutches of goose and duck eggs during the following breeding season.

'In the breeding season, work can finish at any time during the light hours of the evening, depending on the amount of hatchings that require attention. In the winter months, work finishes at 5 pm.

'Prior to the 1972 breeding season we had fifteen potential

breeding pairs of the black brant goose in the breeding area. During March of the year, the winter flock formation started to fragment, and a great deal of aggression was observed as the birds fought over their respective territory. Eight pairs eventually laid, whereupon the eggs were removed and replaced with dummies until each goose had completed laying their clutch. We then replaced the dummy eggs with the eggs from lesser snow goose, whilst the black brant's more precious eggs were incubated under bantams. A total of thirty-five eggs were laid by the eight breeding pairs, thirty-two of which proved to be fertile and hatched. The year in question was a particularly good season for this species of waterfowl, but like all such breeding successes, there are good years and bad years, for no real apparent reason.

'In this type of career, one has to be really dedicated in order to make a success of it. Short cuts just do not work. I try to follow nature's way as closely as possible. I record daily any interesting observations, no matter how irrelevant they may seem at the time; over the months or even years, a pattern or important guideline for the benefit of the species in question may be gleaned from such recordings.

'Finally, as a dedicated animal man, if my instinct tells me to do something with an animal I act immediately, and nine times out of ten my instinct has proved to be right.'

CHAPTER ELEVEN

Wildlife Parks and Dolphinariums

The main objectives behind the running of a zoological institution, which I have outlined in Chapter Ten, should also apply to the wildlife parks and game reserves which have proliferated in Britain in recent years. Providing the more lucrative of these enterprises adopt a positive approach to conservation, and broaden their aims, they will at the same time offer opportunities for a valuable and interesting career working with exotic animals.

THE SAFARI PARK INDUSTRY

During the last decade, an increasing number of Britain's stately homes have used their parklands to provide an environment for herds, prides, troupes and flocks of exotic animals. By doing this the landlord receives a return from his land far in excess to any other usage so far envisaged. The safari park operator has generated a multi-million-pound empire and the general public are under the impression that they are seeing animals in a setting similar to that of their natural wild state.

As a recreational enterprise, the safari park industry undoubtedly offers the public an impressive experience. For a 'home park', with its majestic oaks, beeches and gnarled chestnuts, interlaced with graceful species of antelope, smatterings of lion and flocks of crane provides visitors with a day to remember.

At present, the safari parks' chief merit lies in the exhibition of certain species of the larger exotic animals. I consider this regrettable; for, through its undoubted financial success, the safari park industry possesses an enormous potential for contributing something really worthwhile to the propagation and scientific study of wildlife in general.

It would appear that there is a lack of properly trained personnel in charge of the animals and, in some instances, an absence of suitable winter accommodation for the stock. It is also regrettable that so many safari park directors have had little or no zoological training, and do not belong to the fraternity of people really concerned with animals. As time passes, it is hoped that land agents, builders, hoteliers and ex-circus personnel will confine their activities to the business side of the safari park industry, leaving the animals to the care of professionally trained zoological men.

Management

Mr Stefan Ormrod, who for the last twelve years has been working directly with exotic animals, spent a year as a warden at one of Britain's largest safari parks. He outlines the managerial structure as follows:

The directors have a limited zoological involvement with the running of the individual parks; general managers are responsible to the directors for the daily running of the parks; assistant general managers have little to do with the animals but mainly deal with the accounts, guide books and general public relations.

The warden has limited powers in the running of the park itself, although he is in charge of the day-to-day care of the animals. Due to the great expansion of this industry, experienced wardens are few and far between. Some wardens have had little experience with the species of animals under their care. Assistant wardens act as the wardens' right-hand men.

Head rangers are normally in charge of a section: the lion

section includes lions, tigers, cheetahs; the rhinoceros section includes eland, antelope, wildebeeste, zebra, crowned crane and ostrich, and the monkey jungle section includes baboons, bears and the like. The grouping of species belonging to a section varies from park to park, although in general the same type of animals appear in all cases.

Rangers form the bulk of the animal staff. They are usually given a number denoting their position in a section: eg lion section 1 head ranger, 2 deputy head ranger, 3 his deputy, 4 and so on. After the first few, the numbers become relevant only for radio contact purposes.

In addition to the above, there will be a storeman, a mechanic and safari bus drivers.

A safari park warden's day

During Stefan Ormrod's year as a warden he had the opportunity to make a personal assessment of the validity of the safari park industry in relation to the objectives of some older zoological institutions.

This is his account of a general day's duty as a safari park warden:

08.30 My first duties as warden are to check in all members of the staff and then send them out to their vehicles, after issuing them with guns, ammunition and radios. All vehicles are then checked for fuel and oil, tractors are used as well as Land Rovers. Head rangers take their staff out to their sections.

08.45 I radio all head rangers for preliminary check that sections are staffed and all is well. Should there be a problem, I proceed to the area and try to solve it. I am always on radio call, either with my vehicle radio or hand set. I then proceed to the general manager's office and discuss the day ahead.

09.15 I proceed from 'base' through main gates, and start my inspection of the park. Check with each head ranger that his section is ready, whilst staff are cleaning animal houses and most animals are out in the park.

09.50 By now I am at the farthest point of the park, having driven through every section. I radio to the general manager and tell him the park is ready for opening. I then return to base.

10.05 All head rangers return to my office and hand in their daily report sheets. I check these and sign them, then take them to the general manager who also signs them. The animal report sheets are an excellent idea, but in reality they are a failure. In general, the report consists of comments like 'OK', 'not eating', 'seems all right'. As can be imagined, when a man has to report on seventy baboons in three acres, he is unlikely to know if one has not been eating. When I attempted to go back in time and check previous records, I found comments like 'Rudolph's (Rudolph was a white rhinoceros) wound is much better'. However, search as I might, there was no previous mention of this wound, how it was obtained or what treatment had been prescribed.

A typical report card would read:

SECTION: LION

Animal's name	*Comments*	*Signature*
Walter	OK	
Alice	OK	
Spitfire	OK	
E Type	OK	

As can be seen, the end result is negative, for there is not time to check through 365 pieces of paper for each section in order to glean a few helpful and relevant remarks.

During this time of the day, while the park is open to the public, the patrol men drive round and round, whilst the gap men in charge of the traffic flow and entrance security remain sitting at their respective posts; a few rangers prepare animal feeds.

Lunch relief is arranged for the staff of all sections, apart from the big cat section, where they have to remain on duty throughout the day and lunch has to be delivered to them. All staff get free cooked lunches, and in the summer packed lunches of sandwiches and fruit.

Apart from the general supervision of the animals, on a busy day the staff may have to deal with as many as 200 vehicle breakdowns in the park.

As warden, if any of the animals have to be caught up, require veterinary care, or if other problems present themselves, I have to be present to officiate. The warden also has to keep a constant check on the sections, reprimanding staff for neglecting duties or congratulating staff whenever necessary. Frequently, VIPs have to be taken through the park, and it is sometimes necessary to help organise film work.

18.00 The animals are fed and shut into their sleeping quarters (if they have any). Each section ensures that there are no visitors' cars in their respective areas of the park. A final tour of inspection is made, the staff hand in their guns, ammunition and radios, and check out. I then lock the gates.

A night watchman patrols the park between 21.00 and 06.00 hours.

The average number of staff at this safari park varied between 35 and 40, but was increased during the summer months to help cope with the hordes of visitors.

Further information about openings for people wishing to work in wildlife parks can be obtained from the Secretary, The National Zoological Association, The Woburn Wild Animal Kingdom, Woburn, Bedfordshire.

DOLPHINARIUMS

During my travels, I have seen a varied selection of dolphins in their natural environment as well as in captivity. Some of the species I have observed swimming freely in the vast Amazonian network of rivers in South America, others in dolphinariums in Florida and Europe.

Dolphinariums have only recently become a part of the recreational entertainment scene. At first the life span of the captive dolphin was minimal, but now, thanks to a great increase in pooled knowledge of the dolphin's basic requirements, some of these establishments have become extremely professional. Those who have watched these masterly creatures in action will understand the attraction of working with them. As with all careers in animal management, so much of their success and welfare depends on the quality of the people directly responsible for them.

Mr Martin Padley, dolphin-trainer in charge of the animals at Marineland Côte d'Azur, in France, has contributed his personal experiences with regard to captive dolphins:

If you have ever seen dolphins performing you will no doubt have been impressed and amused by these effervescent animals.

You may have wondered how they are kept and how the trainers achieve the results they do. The training of the dolphins is a small part of the trainer's daily programme. The keeping of the dolphins is in many ways more difficult and time consuming.

A dolphin-trainer's day is always a full and often varied one. However, there are certain routine jobs that must be done to maintain the dolphin in good physical and mental health.

The first job of the day is to inspect all his animals. He must check to see if their eyes are wide open, that they have no infected cuts or swellings, for their skin and eyes are very sensitive and can easily be infected by water-borne bacteria.

Also the trainer has to watch how each dolphin behaves individually and study their interactions to other dolphins in the pool. Each dolphin has its own character and peculiarity, consequently there are occasional clashes of personalities and fights result. By constant observation, the trainer can get to know each one of his animals as an individual and so treat them accordingly.

Just as land mammals in captivity must be kept in hygienic

living quarters so must aquatic mammals. The water that a dolphin lives in must be kept exceptionally clean and sterile if it is to survive the normal life span of thirty or so years. The water is cleaned by sand filters, whilst the sterilisation is attained by adding liquid or gas chlorine.

It is the trainer's responsibility to analyse the chlorine content in the water; this he must do several times a day to assure a safe level. Too much chlorine can be very dangerous, for it can easily burn the dolphins' eyes and skin, and as they drink the pool water their stomach linings can also be affected.

The trainer has to prepare the fish for his dolphins; again hygiene is very important. A dolphin weighing 400lb will easily consume 12–15lb of herring or mackerel a day. To avoid parasites and bacteria the fish is stored at −30° C. When the fish has been completely thawed out, it can be given by the trainer to the dolphins as a 'thank you' or reward for the work they do during the day.

During the deep freezing and eventual thawing of the fish, chemical changes take place and many vital vitamins are lost. To avoid vitamin deficiency, these must be replaced; therefore, every morning before the main meal, the trainer must give the dolphins one or two fishes full of vitamin tablets.

The afternoon is normally 'show time' for the trainer and his students; all that they have learned during the many hours of training is now put into an organised performance.

Dolphins are extremely intelligent as well as being sensitive, and the trainer must always remain patient with them. However, this is not always as easy as it may appear, for the dolphins are great humourists, and frequently make their trainer look foolish by refusing to do the tricks he has taught them. This refusal usually coincides with the particular show being watched by hundreds of people. The nature of the dolphins' frivolity can only be respected.

At the end of the day the trainer's observations, along with water and air temperatures, amounts of fish eaten by each dolphin, and chlorine reading are marked into his log. All this being done, he can say goodnight to his animals knowing that tomorrow they will be the cheeky, happy animals that command every iota of his respect.

CHAPTER TWELVE

Fur Farming

While I can well understand that some people have a substantial amount of enthusiasm for fur farming, it is not a career in which I could find myself directly involved. The breeding of certain species of fur-bearing animals for the sole purpose of stripping them of their pelts appears to me to be a limited field with little glamour attached to it. However, as Mr W. R. Kingston mentioned with regard to the work of animal technicians—which applies equally to fur farming—it is important to have a purposeful attitude towards the whole concept of this type of animal career, for the people involved are faced with the knowledge that the animals in their care will ultimately be put down.

Aesthetically, there appears to be little difference between breeding animals for their pelts and breeding cattle and poultry for their meat. In all cases, the animal is killed in order to yield its contribution for the human race. If this deliberation is accepted, the scientific farming of fur-bearing animals is justifiable, providing that in the process it does not in any way endanger the survival of a species. Fur-bearing animals of the 'spotted cat' group of felines, for example, are grossly exploited and their wild populations devastated for the purpose of pandering to ill-informed fashion. The once ubiquitous leopard is being shot out of Africa approximately 80 per cent faster than its breeding capacity. It is therefore essential that the fur industry confines its activities to skins gleaned from farm-reared progeny.

Few people are aware of the great magnitude of the fur trade as it stands at present. It is one of the world's oldest industries, which began when man utilised furs to provide himself with warm clothing. Primitive man killed animals for food, and it was only natural for him to take the skins and fashion them into some sort of garment. Over the centuries animal furs have become increasingly valuable, not only as protective clothing but as articles of personal adornment, and in some cases of prestige. The smaller mammals, such as the mink, chinchilla, ermine, sable and fox, have now become the luxury furs of the world. These animals are kept and bred on commercial fur farms.

MINK FARMING

Anyone interested in a mink-farming career, with the intention of starting his own farm in the future, is strongly advised to gain some practical experience on a mink farm before investing any capital in such a venture. It has frequently happened that this type of work has turned out to be less appealing than when it was first contemplated.

All mink farmers are advised to join the Fur Breeders Association of the United Kingdom and Ireland, which handles most of the marketing of pelts. The price paid depends very much on the condition of the pelts, so that bundles are graded prior to being auctioned.

On an average-sized mink farm there will be 600–1,000 specimens, in the ratio of one male to five females. Each animal is kept in a separate wire cage unit. Mink breed once a year, the majority of organised matings taking place in March, with litters born during May. They are fully grown at six months when they can be pelted (killed and skin removed); being winter time, their coats are then at their longest and most luxuriant. Those which are not cropped will reach sexual maturity within their first year of life. The males are larger and have coarser fur than the smaller, softer-textured females. Mink are tenacious animals and will bite the handler whenever an opportunity occurs.

Mink are fed only on fresh foodstuffs, so that it is advantageous for a farm to be located near a sea port, a source of cheap and nutritious fodder, where fish heads can be obtained; these are minced prior to feeding. Other foods include minced offal, chicken and lights, while a more expensive synthetic meal is given by some farmers. Foxes, which are also bred for their pelts, are kept by some mink farms. They are more economical to feed, as they will eat foodstuffs not fresh enough to give to the mink.

Perhaps the most interesting facet of mink farming is selective breeding—discovering yearly the number of genetic throw-ups that can be produced. Some of these will arouse more interest in the purchaser, as well as commanding the highest prices. When the mink are killed, the pelts must be prepared, graded into sizes and colours, then made up into lots ready for despatch to the Hudson Bay Company.

Further details about the mink-breeding industry can be obtained from the Secretary, Fur Breeders Association, Beaver Hall, Garlick Hill, London EC4. The association has some ten to twelve area representatives and publishes a bi-monthly journal, *The United Kingdom and Ireland Fur Farmers' Gazette*.

CHINCHILLA RANCHING

Paradoxically, the success of commercial chinchilla farming represents an interesting example of successful conservation.

By 1910, the chinchilla had almost been annihilated throughout its distribution in Bolivia, Chile, Argentina and Peru. When a species declines to this extent, the animal usually becomes extinct, as the odds against its survival from the elements and natural enemies are overwhelming. Realising that the wild supply would die off in a few years, the South American governments concerned permitted the trapping of chinchillas provided the purpose was to raise and propagate them in captivity, thereby saving it from complete extinction. The chinchilla in fact owes its survival to the use of its pelt in the fur trade, on which the vast North American chinchilla industry was founded.

Breeding

A fur-farming operation, whether its chief profits come from the sale of breeding stock or pelts, cannot long continue in business if the animals fail to produce satisfactorily, both in numbers and in the quality of the fur. To secure good reproduction, the fur farmer must start out with foundation breeding stock that has a genetic background of good productivity and quality. He must maintain this productivity and quality by culling out the inevitable inferior offspring and poor producers. He must also ensure that his animals are properly fed, accommodated and handled.

In *Chinchilla Care*, a complete guide to the proper management of a chinchilla ranch, J. W. Houston and J. P. Prestwich point out that foresighted ranchers are interested in more than just good productivity. Fur farming is a business of raising fur. The quality of the fur will in the end determine the price the rancher receives for his stock. The book covers in detail monogamous and polygamous matings, artificial insemination, fur grading, breeding for herd improvement, line-breeding, determining dominant and recessive characteristics, improving mediocre herds, and culling.

Further details about chinchilla ranching in the British Isles, can be obtained from: Mr B. Spooner-Lillingston, Secretary, The Chinchilla Fur Breeders Association Ltd, 64 College Road, Maidstone, Kent ME15 6JJ.

APPENDIX ONE

University Education

Over the broad spectrum of work with animals, I strongly recommend those who have managed to attain a good level of education during their mid-teens to continue their academic studies at university level. A degree will, in the long run, only be advantageous to a chosen career.

I have dealt in some detail with the necessary scholastic attainments for a candidate entering the agriculture industry and the veterinary profession, and for those becoming nursing auxiliaries or animal technicians. To provide more guidelines regarding admission to universities for BSc courses, I am quoting some extracts from the information leaflet ADM/73 published by the Universities Central Council on Admissions (UCCA): obtainable from PO Box 28, Cheltenham, Gloucestershire GL50 1HY (tel 0242 59091).

THE FUNCTIONS OF UCCA

The Universities Central Council on Admissions was set up in 1961 by the universities of the United Kingdom in order to solve some of the problems arising from the increased pressure of applicants for admission.

The duty of the Council is to enable the business of admission to undergraduate courses in all its constituent United Kingdom universities to be dealt with in an orderly manner and, equally important, in a way which gives proper freedom to the individual candidate in making a responsible choice without interfering with the equally proper need of individual universities to select the students they wish to have. It is also the Council's duty to provide statistics arising from its annual operations.

The Council consists of representatives of all the universities in the United Kingdom, except the Open University, together with co-opted members who include heads of schools; its operations are controlled by an executive committee appointed from its own members. Its work is financed by contributions from member universities and administered by a permanent staff from its office in Cheltenham.

UCCA cannot give academic advice, eg about choice of university or course, entrance requirements, scholarships or grants, or an individual candidate's prospects of admission.

In the United Kingdom general information or advice can usually be obtained at school; or from the advisory officer of your local education authority if you have left school; or from the universities. University prospectuses and handbooks, if not available at school, should be obtained from the universities.

THE UCCA SCHEME

The UCCA handbook *How to Apply for Admission to A University* is published annually for use by candidates intending to apply through UCCA during the following academic year. It contains details of admission procedure; the names and addresses of the universities; lists of all the courses for which application must be made through UCCA; and essential instructions on how to complete the UCCA application form.

The UCCA scheme is concerned only with undergraduate courses, ie those leading to a first degree or a first diploma at a university college in the United Kingdom. A first degree is usually a bachelor's degree, eg BA, BSc, LLB; but in Scotland the MA is a first degree.

Entrance requirements

To be considered for admission to a university you must not only satisfy the 'general' requirement for the particular university concerned but also the 'course' requirement. The 'general' requirement represents the minimum admission standard laid down by the individual university, usually expressed in terms of passes in the GCE examination. In addition universities specify conditions which must be satisfied for admission to a particular course (ie the 'course' requirement) to ensure that the candidate is academically qualified for the course in question. Satisfying the general and course requirements does not of itself ensure admission. The number of applicants each year who satisfy these requirements is greater than the number of places available, so there is considerable competition for entry. The extent of the competition differs from university to university and from subject to subject. All decisions about admission are made by universities individually. University selectors may take into account factors other than examination performance including, for example, the confidential report from the head of the school or in some cases impressions formed at interview of the candidate's depth of interest in his chosen subject—but so far as examination performance is concerned it is generally true that the better a candidate's results in the school-leaving examination, the better his or her chances of admission. Candidates usually apply through UCCA in the autumn before they take public examinations in the following summer; and to selected candidates the universities may make conditional offers, specifying the grades needed in the required subjects.

Details of general course requirements are given in *A Compendium of University Entrance Requirements for First Degree Courses in the United Kingdom*. This is published by the Association of Commonwealth Universities for the Committee of Vice-Chancellors and Principals and available from Lund Humphries, The Country Press, Drummond Road, Bradford BD8 8DH, Yorkshire. It is essential to use only the current edition of this compendium. A table showing the minimum age of entry to university is also given.

Please do not write to UCCA about entrance requirements. Full details of the general requirements at the various universities should be obtained from the registrar, secretary or admissions officer of the university or college concerned.

Where to obtain information

Consult the universities if you wish to know whether your qualifications will exempt you from part of the course for which you intend to apply. Exemption from the first year of an undergraduate degree course does not entitle you to apply direct; application must be made through UCCA.

For information about details of syllabuses of the courses offered at universities; scholarships, fees and accommodation; your possible chances of success—ask the universities concerned.

For information about grants—write to your local education authority; scholarships—the universities to which you intend to apply; industrial awards—the firms or institutions concerned. Scottish candidates should write to the Scottish Education Department, Awards Branch, 2 Charlotte Street, Edinburgh EH2 4AP for information about student allowances.

When to apply

For October 1974 entry, for example, your application must reach UCCA between 1 September 1973 and the closing date of 15 December 1973. But if Oxford or Cambridge are included in your choice, your application must reach UCCA by the closing date of 15 October 1973, and you must before then (by 30 September 1973) submit a preliminary form to one or both of the universities.

Address inquiries about admission to Cambridge to: The Tutor for Admissions, —— College, Cambridge.

You must apply to one of the colleges and not to the university. Your headmaster or headmistress will have a copy of the *Cam-*

bridge Admissions Prospectus. Alternatively the Cambridge Intercollegiate Applications Office, 4A Benett Street, Cambridge CB2 3QN (or any college) will send you a copy on application.

Address inquiries about admission to Oxford to: The Tutor for Admissions, —— College, Oxford.

Admission at Oxford is to one of the colleges. Your headmaster or headmistress should have copies of booklets describing the admission procedure, or they may be obtained from the Oxford Colleges, Admissions Office, 58 Banbury Road, Oxford OX2 6PP.

Deferred entry

Universities may consider you during 1973–4 for admission in October 1975 if (a) you intend to leave school before September 1974; and (b) *either* you need to be sure of a university place in order to carry out your plans for 1974–5, eg you wish to take a course of pre-university training in industry; *or* you will be abroad and not available for interview, eg in voluntary service overseas.

If in doubt consult each university or college before you apply. Candidates accepted for entry in 1975 must not subsequently apply to other universities in the 1974–5 admissions scheme.

INDUSTRIAL TRAINING (UK CANDIDATES)

If you are interested in combining or alternating university study with industrial training, consult the university as well as the firm before you apply through UCCA. The Central Youth Employment Executive publishes a summary of awards (14) made by industrial and professional organisations and there is a UCCA leaflet (15) which explains how and when to apply.

Other branches of education outside the UCCA scheme about which UCCA is frequently asked include diploma or certificate courses of one year's duration or less, postgraduate courses, teacher training courses, Open University courses, to mention only a few. Addresses where information can be obtained about these are listed in the UCCA information leaflets.

APPENDIX TWO

Useful Addresses

PART ONE

DOGS

The Bellmead Kennelmaid Training School, Priest Hill House, Priest Hill, Old Windsor, Berkshire

The Guide Dogs for the Blind Association, 113 Uxbridge Road, Ealing, London W5 5TQ

The Kennel Club, 1 Clarges Street, London W1

National Greyhound Racing Association, The Hook Kennels, Northaw, Nr Potters Bar, Hertfordshire

(*military dogs*)

Deputy Assistant Director, Army Veterinary Services, The War Office (V & R), Droitwich, Worcestershire

(*police dogs*)

Officer-in-Charge, Hampshire Police Dog Section, Chief Constable's Office, Headquarters, Winchester SO22 5DB

CATS

The Hon Secretary, Feline Advisory Board, 18 Jephtha Road, Wandsworth, London SW18 1QH

The Secretary, Governing Council of the Cat Fancy, Dovefield, Petwood Road, Witley, Surrey GU8 5QW

HORSES

The British Horse Society, National Equestrian Centre, Stoneleigh, Kenilworth, Warwickshire CV8 2LR

Careers Office, Household Cavalry, Combermere Barracks, Windsor, Berkshire SL4 3DN

Metropolitan Police, Mounted Police Training Establishment, Imber Court, East Molesey, Surrey

Ponies of Britain, Brookside Farm, Winkfield Row, Ascot, Berkshire (*governing body of pony trekking centres*)

PART TWO

AGRICULTURE

Agricultural Education Association, Staffordshire College of Agriculture, Rodbaston, Penkridge, Staffordshire

Agricultural Training Board, Bourne House, 32/4 Beckenham Road, Beckenham, Kent BR3 4PB

Royal Agricultural Society of England, 35 Belgrave Square, London SW1

Royal Highland and Agricultural Society of Scotland, 8 Eglinton Crescent, Edinburgh 12

Royal Welsh Agricultural Society, Llanelwedd, Buith Wells, Breconshire

Women's Farm and Garden Association, Courtauld House, Byng Place, London WC1

POULTRY

British Federation of Poultry Industries, High Holborn House, 52/4 High Holborn, London WC1

National Poultry Diploma Board Ltd, Golden Buffs, Burney Bit, Pamber Heath, Basingstoke, Hampshire

(*game birds*)

The Game Conservancy, Fordingbridge, Hampshire

PART THREE

VETERINARY

Army Veterinary and Remount Services, The Ministry of Defence, Droitwich, Worcestershire

Careers Research and Advisory Centre, Bateman Street, Cambridge

Royal College of Veterinary Surgeons, 32 Belgrave Square, London SW1X 9QP

NURSING AUXILIARIES

Royal College of Veterinary Surgeons, 32 Belgrave Square, London SW1X 8QP

ANIMAL TECHNICIANS

Institute of Animal Technicians, (Registered Office) 16 Beaumont Street, Oxford OX1 2LZ

NATURE CONSERVATION

International Union for Conservation of Nature and National Resources (IUCN), 1110 Morges, Switzerland

The Jersey Wildlife Preservation Trust (JWPT), Les Augrès Manor, Trinity, Jersey, Channel Islands

The Nature Conservancy, 19–20 Belgrave Square, London SW1X 8PY

The Society for the Promotion of Nature Reserves (SPNR), The Manor House, Alford, Lincolnshire

ANIMAL WELFARE

Royal Society for the Prevention of Cruelty to Animals (RSPCA), The Manor House, Horsham, Sussex RH2 1HG

PART FOUR

ZOOS

The Federation of Zoological Gardens of Great Britain and Ireland, Zoological Gardens, Regent's Park, London NW1 4RY

The National Zoological Association, The Woburn Wild Animal Kingdom, Woburn, Bedfordshire

FUR FARMING

Chinchilla Fur Breeders Association Ltd, 64 College Road, Maidstone, Kent ME15 6JJ

The Fur Breeders Association, Beaver Hall, Garlick Hill, London EC4

APPENDIX ONE

UNIVERSITIES

Universities Central Council on Admissions (UCCA), PO Box 28, Cheltenham, Gloucestershire GL50 1HY

The Universities Federation for Animal Welfare (UFAW), 7A Lamb's Conduit Passage, London WC1

APPENDIX THREE

Further Reading

PART ONE

DOGS

Dog World (magazine and yearbook)
The Dog World Ltd, 32 New Street, Ashford, Kent

Our Dogs (magazine and yearbook)
Our Dogs Publishing Co Ltd, Oxford Road, Station Approach, Manchester M60 1SX

CATS

Bulletin of the Feline Advisory Board (quarterly)
The Hon Secretary, Feline Advisory Board, 18 Jephtha Road, Wandsworth, London SW18 1QH

Cats and Cat Care International Encyclopaedia
Eds G. N. Henderson and D. J. Coffey (Newton Abbot: David & Charles, 1973)

HORSES

A Career with Horses
Published by The British Horse Society, National Equestrian Centre, Kenilworth, Warwickshire CV8 2LP

The Horse's Health from A to Z
P. D. Rossdale and S. M. Wreford (Newton Abbot: David & Charles, 1974)

Work with Horses as a Career
Dorian Williams (London: Batsford, 1963)

PART TWO

AGRICULTURE AND POULTRY

Agriculture, Fisheries, Food (catalogue of departmental publications)
Ministry of Agriculture, Fisheries & Food (Publications), Tolcarne Drive, Pinner, Middlesex HAS 2DT

Catalogue of publications dealing with all aspects of agriculture obtainable from:
The Library, Ministry of Agriculture, Fisheries & Food, Whitehall Place, London SW1 3HH

PART THREE

VETERINARY

A Career as a Veterinary Surgeon
Published by The Royal College of Veterinary Surgeons, 32 Belgrave Square, London SW1X 8QP

Veterinary Science Degree Course Guide
Published by the Careers Research and Advisory Centre, Bateman Street, Cambridge

NURSING AUXILIARIES

A Guide for Persons Wishing to Train as Registered Animal Nursing Auxiliaries
Published by the Royal College of Veterinary Surgeons, 32 Belgrave Square, London SW1X 8QP

ANIMAL TECHNICIANS

Journal of The Institute of Animal Technicians
G. D. Searle & Co Ltd (Miss B. F. Whatley, FIAT, editor), Lane End Road, High Wycombe, Buckinghamshire

CONSERVATION

Animals Magazine (monthly)
21–2 Great Castle Street, London W1N 8LT

Careers in the Nature Conservancy
The Nature Conservancy, 19–20 Belgrave Square, London SW1X 8PY

Oryx
Journal of The Fauna Preservation Society, c/o Zoological Society of London, Regent's Park, London NW1 4RY

World Wildlife Fund Yearbook
1110 Morges, Switzerland

PART FOUR

ZOOS

The International Zoo News Magazine
Ed Geoffrey Schomberg, Zoological Gardens, Regent's Park, London NW1 4RY

The International Zoo Yearbook
Ed Nicole Duplaix Hall, published by The Zoological Society of London, Regent's Park, London NW1 4RY

APPENDIX ONE

UNIVERSITY

Handbook on the Care and Management of Laboratory Animals
The Universities Federation for Animal Welfare (UFAW), 7A Lamb's Conduit Passage, London WC1

Acknowledgements

A book of this nature could never be as comprehensive and include such a cross-section of individual experience in various careers with animals without the assistance of many people. It is therefore my duty and pleasure to acknowledge the unstinted help received in abundance from many friends and correspondents.

I am grateful to the following individuals for offering advice as well as providing me with information concerning specific subjects: Mr T. Collier (boarding kennels), Miss N. Day (boarding kennels), Mr J. Mallet (breeding dogs), Mr A. J. Phillipson (guide dogs), Lt-Colonel J. R. Spurry (military dogs and horses), Inspector J. Moore (police dogs), Mr P. Scott (greyhounds), Mrs J. Mallet (cat breeding), Colonel N. Grove-White (British Horse Society), Mr and Mrs F. B. Finnis (riding stables), Chief Superintendent A. F. Pilder (police horses), Major C. W. J. Lewis (military horses), Mr N. Hicks (Agricultural Training Board), Mr J. Craven (game birds), the Royal Veterinary College, Mrs J. I. Plumb (nursing auxiliaries), Mr G. A. Thomson (animal technicians), Mr D. Harris (animal technician), Miss B. Mason (the Nature Conservancy), Mr N. Phillips (county naturalists' trusts), Mrs V. Dakowski and Mr L. P. Flint (RSPCA), Mr G. St G. Schomberg (zoos), Mr C. Marler (waterfowl), Dr M. Brambell (zoo mammals and veterinary), Mr D. J. B. Copp (biology), Dr R. D. Martin (zoology), Mr C. Bertram (mink farming), Mrs B. Burgess (university entrance).

My special thanks are due to the specialists who have provided me with first-hand accounts describing the nature of their particular work with animals: Mr N. Albright (guide-dog mobility instructor), Inspector L. Goodall (officer-in-charge, Hampshire police dog section), Miss S. M. Hamilton Moore (proprietor, cat boarding establishment), Mrs F. Roden (cat breeder), Mrs S. Elsie (racing stables), Mr N. Surridge (owner, broiler-breeding farm), Mr D. Jemson (veterinary surgeon), Miss M. Collins (registered animal nurse), Mr W. R. Kingston (chief animal technician), Mr C. Heath (chief inspector RSPCA), Mr D. Riordan (in charge of small mammals, Jersey Zoo), Mr T. B. Kichenside (head keeper, London Zoo), Mr R. Ainsley (curator of reptiles, Chester Zoo), Mr S. Ormrod (ex-warden, safari park), Mr M. Padley (in charge of dolphinarium).

My thanks to Mrs E. Gruchy for her forbearance in having to type and retype from some untidy manuscripts during the preparation of the diverse information contained in this book, and my gratitude to Mr Gerald Durrell for his guidance in my chosen career with animals and for writing the Foreword to this book.

Index

Index